8²

02/01/02

KAPLAN

Dear Moll

This looks interesting, too.
Just a few minutes a day for the
rest of your life...

Haven't heard from you.

Dada

Power Up!
other Kaplan Power Books:

Grammar Power
Math Power
Writing Power

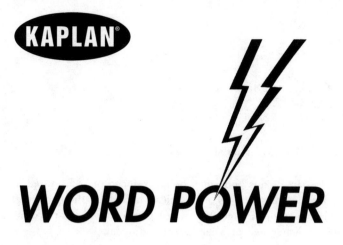

WORD POWER

by Meg F. Schneider

SIMON & SCHUSTER

Kaplan Books
Published by
Kaplan Educational Centers and Simon & Schuster
1230 Avenue of the Americas
New York, NY 10020

Production Editor: Maude Spekes
Cover Design: Amy McHenry
Interior Page Design: Bola Famuyiwa
Production Coordinator: Gerard Capistrano
Managing Editors: Kiernan McGuire and Brent Gallenberger
Executive Editor: Jay Johnson
Special thanks to:
Martha Arango, Jennifer Bacon, Roseann Lloyd, and Julie Schmidt

Manufactured in the United States of America
Published simultaneously in Canada

July 1997
10 9 8 7 6 5 4 3 2

Library of Congress Cataloging-in-Publication Data
Schneider, Meg F.
    Word power / Meg F Schneider.
        P.cm
    ISBN 0-684-84154-1
    1. Vocabulary—Problems, exercises, etc.   I. Title.
PE1449.S345 1997   97-13089
428.1--DC21   CIP

ISBN 0-684-84154-1

TABLE OF CONTENTS

SECTION 3: REALLY HARD WORDS YOU OUGHT TO KNOW

MEG F. SCHNEIDER is the author of many parenting and self-help titles as well as fiction and nonfiction books for teens. She is also a New York City based book packager, specializing in relationships, parenting and family living subjects. She holds an M.A. in Counselling Psychology from Columbia University and is the mother of two young boys.

The Power of *Word Power* Lessons

We couldn't include in this book every word in the English language. We assume you know that! What we did attempt to do was organize the most important words into three broad categories (falling into the three sections of this book). We started in section 1 with the words you really ought to know already—to build your confidence and to straighten out any critical incorrect impressions you might have had about actual meanings. (For example, *fidelity* is not simply the name of a mutual fund—see Lesson 7.) If you know these words, we figure you're ready to have lunch with an admissions counselor at Harvard or make a great impression during your human resources interview at a Fortune 500 firm. Sections 2 and 3 cover words with increasing difficulty. You'll wind up training your brain and increasing your word power with each new level you decide to tackle.

Keep these lesson features in mind as you use Kaplan's *Word Power*:

We didn't overdo the usage examples. Other vocabulary-building books do that, and it's confusing. We get you in and we get you out. To learn the words so that they stick, you need to learn the basic definition and usage, and then go out and hear the word used in regular conversation (i.e., our sample sentences). That's how you learn proper usage. The logic for this plan for learning is incontrovertible (see Lesson 10).

We tip you off to the hot test words. Look for the lightning bolt; it shows up next to a word often found on the SAT, GRE, or other standardized test. You might find any of the words in this book on those tests, but the ones marked with the little lightning bolt frequently appear. But again, don't study only the "hot test words" (unless you're in a panic to study!). The people who create standardized tests will change the vocabulary items off and on.

We help you say difficult words correctly. We include the phonetic pronunciation in cases when a word could easily be mispronounced. We've broken it down into familiar sounds and spelled it out in syllables. If you're not sure about how to pronounce a word, ask an erudite friend. If you don't have any, don't use the word until you hear someone else use it (and make sure it's someone "smart"). You should remember, too, that people in different geographic regions may prounounce words differently from one another. *Banal,* one of the words in this book, has more than one pronunciation. Smart people talk like the smart people in their own region. So, perk up your ears and pay attention!

We tip you off to multiple parts of speech. In many instances we've given you a few forms of a word so that you have a sense of how a word in one part of speech, say, a noun, can be changed slightly and used as another, like an adjective or adverb. (Don't worry. This is called "getting something for free." We're not charging you for the variants.)

We challenge you to learn word meanings. The lesson quizzes (which we call "Plug In") will occasionally try to trip you up, to see if you will incorrectly match a word with a definition, for no other reason than "it rings a bell." We did this by offering similar definitions for several words, so that you can't just think to yourself, "Oh, yeah . . . I remember reading that definition in this lesson." Rather, you'll have to actually think about which word makes the correct match. You may see this as a trick, but consider it as a device that forces you to think about nuances of meaning. This process will deepen your learning. (Note: For easy reference, we put the answers to the quizzes right after each quiz.)

Powerful learning idea: Every lesson tells a story! When you read the sample sentences for each vocabulary word, note how all the sample sentences for all the words in each lesson form a little story. And note how each lesson is titled, and that title is the title for the story. We did this on purpose. It's that mnemonics thing. We stated earlier that you'll remember words best when you make up your own memory tricks. Still, associating a word in your head with one of our stories may help bring to mind the meaning of a word you might otherwise have forgotten. We believe the stories will strengthen your mental images of the words they include. In fact we're sure of it! We've also organized each lesson around one letter of the alphabet. We encourage you to make your own tongue twisters to connect new words with other words you already know.

So You Want a Power Vocabulary

You may think that improving your vocabulary will carry a high profit margin. You can make an impression with important people. People at parties will view you as erudite. Smart. Someone to know and admire. You can score big at SAT* time. Suddenly those C pluses you've been earning will pale next to the 700 plus scores you receive. You think maybe you can cash in at the workplace. Your employers will assume you are an effective communicator and a boon to the company. (This will be especially true if your employers are insecure and don't understand a word you're saying.)

And romantically? Well, that all depends on whether your date or significant other has an equally ambitious vocabulary, whether polysyllabic words have a seductive effect. Some people like being with someone who sounds smarter than they do. After all, everyone has his own amorous triggers. It would seem, though, that learning a bunch of big fancy words with lots of syllables will set you up for life.

Right? Not exactly.

Why Big Words Aren't Everything

The aim of a strong vocabulary should *not* be to impress other people. The goal of building a powerful vocabulary is *to find the words that say exactly what you mean*, in a manner that can be understood by those who are listening to you.

Even if you learn many more big words and you use them correctly, they may not be understood by your listener. What's the point of that? Big words—uncommon, rarely used, unfamiliar, or fancy words—are not always understood. (For the record, we're using *fancy* because that's what people often say when confronted with a speaker who has a proclivity for unnecessarily complicated conversation. "My, don't you talk fancy," we might say with no small amount of sarcasm.)

Big, fancy words can create a tension-filled atmosphere, making it difficult for people to converse at all. They may give an exchange a formal ring—an anxiety-producing effect. This is because a large part of good communication has to do with creating a kind of intimacy. Big words may cause people to draw back from you. This is as true person to person, as it is speaker to audience. This intimacy is established through your choice of words, which convey both your thoughts, as well as the attitudes and feelings behind them. The fact is you can use technically correct words, but in so doing, convey an impression you don't intend.

Case in point: A co-worker approaches you with a solution to a problem. You think it won't work. You could say, "It's inefficacious to try and work this imbroglio out in such a fashion," but you'll sound like a superior snot. Or, you could try the more prosaic, "I think it's futile for us to try to work the problem out this way," and sound frustrated but companionable. In short, by flinging around a lot of fancy words, you run the risk of losing your co-worker (not to mention friends or your partner), no matter that your words were basically accurate. Now, what do we mean by "basically"?

Nuance Is Everything

nuance n. A subtle or slight degree of difference, as in meaning, color, or tone.

Nuance expresses not just the global point but the specific one as well. A simple example:

> Elizabeth cackled at the look on her brother's face.

> Elizabeth chuckled at the look on her brother's face.

Both *cackled* and *chuckled* are basically correct. This means they both potentially make sense. But they convey a subtle difference.

Let's go to the dictionary. (Not that it's the be-all, and end-all, which we'll get to later.)

cackle v. To make the shrill cry characteristic of a hen after laying an egg. n. Shrill, brittle laughter.

chuckle v. To laugh quietly or to oneself. To cluck, or chuck as a hen. n. A quiet laugh of mild amusement or satisfaction

Now, if Elizabeth had some hidden agenda causing her to receive something other than genuine pleasure from the look on her brother's face, than *cackle* would be fine. But if Elizabeth sincerely felt amused by her brother's expression, then *chuckle* is the way to go. The nuance of the word needs to fit the nuance of the context.

 **Nuances on the SAT and GRE.** Knowing the basic definition of a word will be extremely helpful on the SATs and GRE. It will certainly eliminate options A and B (and if you're lucky, E), though it might leave you torn between C and D. What a nuisance, that nuance. Even in a test situation you may find yourself getting tripped up by the subtle meanings between words as they apply to context. Example:

> It was difficult to imagine Ellen, a _____ woman, as a psychologist; listening while others talked was not her style.
>
> (A) voluble
>
> (B) boorish
>
> (C) pessimistic
>
> (D) truculent
>
> (E) depressed

On this test question, you realize that you're looking for a word that indicates Ellen is a bad listener. That knocks out *pessimistic, truculent,* and *depressed.* Now you have *boorish* (insensitive) and *voluble.* Both might fit, but someone could be boorish without ignoring people, and there's nothing in the sentence to indicate she's a lout. It's clear she'd simply rather do the talking. *Voluble* means talkative. So there you are.

Certainly, when you are speaking, hoping to be understood, you will want to choose the word with the correct nuance as often as possible. And sometimes that word will be neither a long one, nor a seemingly interesting one. Look for the concise word for your meaning.

The Risks of Undisciplined Vocabulary Usage

When you start learning the definitions of some new words, we wouldn't advise employing them until you've heard them used many times, and have a clear and precise sense of what they mean. Otherwise you could sound like a moron. Or worse, a pretentious, insecure jerk. Here are some common faux pas and our suggestions for ways to fix them.

- You might mispronounce the word. This is perfectly awful. The listener will get all caught up wondering if you know you made a mistake, if he should tell you, if you'll get irritated once he does, perhaps you're not so well spoken after all, and before you know it, he won't hear a word you have to say.

- You might misuse the word. This is a particularly egregious mistake. The listener will get all caught up wondering if you know you made a mistake, if he should tell you, will you get irritated if he does, about how smart you are after all, why you are so insecure you have to use words you clearly don't understand — and before you know it, he won't hear a word you have to say. This is probably just as well, since you're not saying what you intend anyway.

- You might use the word technically correctly but in the wrong situation to the wrong person, thereby completely turning off your listener. We're thinking of the doctor who was ambling through the park with a nonmedical friend along with each of their respective children. The doctor's son suddenly banged his head on a tree, and after feeling the child's skull, the doctor commented somberly, "Yes, a significant hematoma." The friend nodded, feeling significantly put off. The kid, he thought, has a big bump. I need this? The doctor's friend promptly developed a hemicrania (a headache).

The Etiquette of Vocabulary Ignorance

You may give the impression that you are a devoted wordsmith, with an impressive vocabulary, thus opening the door for your listener to use some fancy words of her own that you won't understand. Then what?

What to Do When Someone Uses a Word You Don't Know. We suggest saying, with a forthright air, "I don't know that one. Could you define the word?" The implication is that you already know tons. The impression is that you're therefore not embarrassed to not know this one. And the result is that you will escape looking like a charlatan, by the integument of your teeth.

What to Do When Your Listener Asks for a Word Meaning. Don't say, "You're kidding?!" or, "You don't know what that word means?" All of us have holes in our knowledge base. The name of the game is, Get Past the Moment Quickly Because Your Listener is Probably a Little Embarrassed. Simply say, "It means . . ." Then don't add, "You see?" Assume he does. Just move on with your remarks.

What to Do If You Make a Mistake While Speaking. Our vote? Admit the mistake. Say, "You know, I don't think that was the right word." Then quickly choose a less pretentious word and keep speaking. Don't belabor the mistake. Self-admonishments, such as "How could I have done that!" or "I am a jerk," will only underline your discomfort and put your mistake in neon lights. Expressing your awareness of the gaffe will cut off your listener's private litany and help the two of you get on with it.

If you mispronounce a word, try a bit of light humor. "Hmm . . . that didn't sound right. Is it . . . ?" Bring your listener in. It will make her feel smart. It will make you appear self-aware. And it will leave you looking confident—not afraid to elicit the help of others for fear that it will diminish you. Your listener doesn't have to know this is a big trick and you actually feel pathetic. Then, on the other hand, maybe you don't feel bad. Maybe you're thrilled to be learning new words; maybe you're determined to move forward even if you make a few mistakes along the way.

To Avoid the Pitfalls of an Expanding Vocabulary. First, read this book cover to cover. (This is a semiserious suggestion.) Or you can follow these surefire tips:

- It's important to understand you don't need to use a word others won't readily understand in order to sound intelligent. True intelligence comes across when smart thoughts are expressed with clarity, and for the most part, brevity. It's the old "less is more" philosophy.

- Believe that a well-used, simple word will be as effective as a properly used, fancy word, pronounced correctly to the right person.

- And whatever you do, when you are speaking, use only those words you are completely sure of.

Back to Big Tests: What If You Don't Know a Word?

Vocabulary is usually tested in the context of a sentence. That's some help right there. The trick is, you have to find and use the clues. You have to be a detective. Here's how it works in the following sample test sentence.

> Criminals who show remorse are given lighter sentences than those who show no compunction.

Okay. So you have no idea what *compunction* means. But look at the sentence. Criminals who show remorse get a good thing. But those who show no compunction don't. So it stands to reason that *remorse* and *compunction* must mean pretty much the same thing. That's the clue. If *remorse* indicates shame or guilt, then *compunction* probably does too. Therefore "no compunction" would have to mean no shame, no guilt.

Another example:

> Peter had often heard that his photographs were similar to those of a well-established photographer; and so he worried his new, innovative portfolio might also be considered:
>
> (A) typical
>
> (B) formless
>
> (C) derivative
>
> (D) incompetent
>
> (E) suggestive

Peter's past photographs reminded people of someone else's. Peter's worried this will be true of his new stuff, too. A good clue is *innovative*. He's thinking this will stand in the way of his being thought of as a, b, c, d, or e. That knocks out *incompetent*. No one said his work is bad. *Typical* doesn't make sense. Typical of what? *Formless* has nothing to do with it. So you're left with *derivative* or *suggestive*. This is where you might just have to guess. Or you could say to yourself "suggestive"? That would indicate his work suggests someone else's, but it doesn't have to mean that. It could suggest anything. The solar system for example. The only word left is *derivative*. Through the process of elimination, you've flexed your word power on a standardized test. (By the way, the dictionary definition of *derivative* is "to derive, or obtain from a parent source.")

What's Word Power?

We believe that words are learned both through straight definition and through context, and through all forms of "tricks" and practice. We believe that you need to be motivated both by your desire to know more about words, and the sense that your knowledge base is indeed growing.

You need to use (all or in any combination) your eyes, ears, voice, humor, sense of the absurd, reasoning skills, and even handwriting to learn the full meaning and application of a word. (Also how to pronounce it.)

Tips and Tricks for Making Vocabulary Stick

Here is a quick list of some of the ways you can make the words in this book your own. That ability to make new words "stick" is what we mean by "word power." We hope you'll try out all of these tricks and see which ones help you best. Then use them powerfully!

- **Reading** helps you figure out basically what a word means from its context. Remember, though, it's the subtleties that count when speaking or writing. Context does not convey the full scope of meaning, and in fact can be misleading. What if the word is being used sarcastically? Example:

  "Well," James eyed Marissa's dress with disapproval. "Isn't that just sublime."

- **Mnemonics** help as global hints to the meaning of a word, and are often easier to remember than the definition (or fact) itself. This is partly because they have entertainment value. Many students are taught to remember the difference between the word *principle* and *principal* by being told, "The principal is your pal." This of course strikes most kids as absurd, which helps them remember, and gets us to our next point.

- **Absurd imagery** (pictures) can help you remember meanings. Take the word *flout:* to disregard with disrespect. We imagine a strictly religious family Thanksgiving dinner where a floozy (FL) is being told to get out (OUT), for in that traditional family world, no one respects a floozy. Whenever your mind gives you a picture, you will likely remember the word. Your pictures and association will stay with you. This is why this book will not give you any of those kinds of associations. They wouldn't work. The point is for you to make up pictures from your own experience.

- **Etymology** is a solid way to figure out a word. The etymology of a word is its root. Take PED (foot) for instance. PEDal, PEDestrian, exPEDite. These words all have something to do with the foot. All these words have to do with getting somewhere.

- **Writing,** the act of physically putting the word down on paper, helps to solidify it in a person's mind. Writing the word helps our minds remember. Use flash cards. Use bright markers. Write down the word and its definition. Put it in a sentence. Read it over. Test yourself. Take out the cards that give you trouble. Keep writing and practicing to build your word power.

- **Tongue twisters** are childish games that can imprint the meanings of words into grown-up brains. Remember that old one, "Peter Piper picked a peck of pickled peppers"? You may not know the word *peck*, but when you say the tongue twister, it is obvious that *peck* is a quantity, a measurement. As you read the words in each lesson of this book, you can make up your own tongue twisters with the words, for they almost always use the same letter of the alphabet. For example, Lesson 12 has almost all M words:

Morose Mavis made herself into a martyr. "Better a mercenary maverick," she moaned. This may not have the zing of Mother Goose, but it will get you through to the meanings.

How to Put Your Word Power Into Action

Here's our plan. The 750 words we cover in this book (along with many others we'll correct, clarify, and analyze throughout) are divided into three sections:

Section 1 is called "Words to the First Power: Words You Really Ought to Know" (or "Are You Ready to Lunch with the Harvard Admissions Counselor?"). Twenty lessons and twenty sets of lesson quizzes will help you plug in to your first level of word power.

Section 2 is called "Words to the Second Power: Harder Words You Ought to Know" (or "You May Be Ready to Have Coffee with Your Professor"). Another twenty lessons and twenty sets of lesson quizzes will amp up your word power to an even higher level of accomplishment.

Section 3 is called "Words to the Third Power: Really Hard Words You Ought To Know" (or "You Are Ready to Dine with the President of Harvard"). Whoa! You're really supercharging your vocabulary when you cover the fifteen lessons and quiz sets in this final section.

In each *Word Power* lesson, we'll give you the straight definition and part of speech for each vocabulary word. Whenever we hit a word that is commonly found on SATs and GREs, it will be marked with a lightning bolt—study these first if you're in a rush to ace the verbal part of your exam! We'll use the words in a few different forms, in sentences, so that you can get a sense for context. And as we've already warned you, after each lesson you will have a brief Plug In quiz.

Following all the word lessons, we'll give you a chapter that will provide more foundational information to further your word studies. This chapter, titled "Root Juice," is a discussion of etymology. Knowing the roots is an added plus, and they can get you guessing word meanings intelligently when you're faced with a written word you just don't know.

Sounds like a lot, right? But you can work at your own pace.

Don't Zap Your Brain

It's hard to learn vocabulary from a dictionary or thesaurus. *Word Power* is not a dictionary or thesaurus. We're talking real life here. We want to empower you with a vocabulary you can fully understand and use. We want you to ace your standardized test or have a great vocabulary for the workplace.

Dictionaries are great, but they're often hard to understand. For one thing, they try to tell you how to pronounce a word, but unless you know the meaning of a lot of symbols, you can get awfully confused. Second, they do reveal all the meanings of a word, but rarely in any sort of context.

Thesauruses have another problem. They can be quite misleading. Too many readers assume the words listed after the key word mean precisely what that key word means, which is utterly untrue. The words are only possible alternatives. The people who put the thesaurus together have no idea what you want an alternative for, so they cover their bases by giving you all sorts of possibilities. You're supposed to choose the one that best works for you. Here's an example:

> exacerbate v. 1. aggravate, worsen, add insult to injury, intensify, heighten. 2. embitter, gall, ramble, acerbate, sour, poison. 3. exasperate, discompose, distress, ruffle, roil, pique, chafe, grate
>
> Willie *exacerbated* the situation by lying when he was caught cheating.
>
> Willie *heightened* the situation by lying when he was caught cheating.

Which works best? Not *heightened*. *Heightened* speaks to mounting intensity. That's not wrong, but it's not the golden fleece either. It doesn't quite mean "gets worse." *Exacerbated* does.

But how do you know what word works best for you? You read this book. Then when you look up a word in a thesaurus, you'll murmur as you run your eyes over the list, "Nope, not quite what I mean. Ah . . . yes, I forgot about that word. That fits."

In other words don't ever use a thesaurus to teach you how to use a new word. You need to bring what you know about the word to bear on your decision.

A Final Note on Using New Vocabulary Words

You know that line, "It's better to look good than to feel good"? This is, of course, a pathetic approach to life. Well, similarly, it's not better to sound good when in truth you don't know what you're talking about! So be honest with yourself. Don't throw big words around unless you're sure of what they mean!

Sure, some people who know as much or less than you will be impressed, but so what? You'll know. And the more you know the unhappy truth, the more insecure you'll feel, while at the same time learning absolutely nothing except that you can fool some of the people some of the time.

So try to keep this in mind. When it comes to vocabulary of any level, what matters most is that you make sense, that you say what you mean. You don't have to mean what you say of course, but that's an entirely different issue.

What does word power all boil down to? Make sure, even as you stretch your mind and vocabulary, that you maintain healthy respect for little words. The simple words. The words you readily use and easily understand. When you are truly familiar with the less common words, begin to use them judiciously. Carefully. With thought. And discipline.

Communicating is an art. It's a power art. Words are the medium. Do not treat them with disrespect. Your ability to communicate will deepen and broaden. You will express yourself more clearly in the world.

SECTION 1

Words to the First Power: Words You Really Ought to Know

Would You Abdicate or Advocate?

ABDICATE v. to step down from a position of power

> The king decided to *abdicate* in favor of his smart, though woefully impetuous son.

> The *abdication* (n.) heralded a new era.

ABRIDGE v. to shorten, condense, or lessen in length

> At first he planned a lengthy abdication (adj.) speech, but then he decided to give an *abridged* (adj.) version so he wouldn't bore his kingdom to death.

> Had he not decided to *abridge* (v.) the speech himself, the queen was planning to lose it.

ABSOLVE v. to forgive or free from blame

> As part of the king's historic decision, he decided to *absolve* all those villains who languished in the tower.

ABYSMAL adj. (A-BIZ-MAL) extremely wretched, bottomless

> The prisoners had been living in an *abysmal* situation.

ACQUIESCE v. (AK-WEE-ESS) to comply passively, to give in

> The king's cabinet did not easily *acquiesce* to the pardons.

> Their *acquiescence* (n.) was critical.

 Lightning bolt indicates words that frequently appear on the SAT and GRE

ADVOCATE v. to support, or be in favor of

Not one cabinet member could *advocate* (v.) the king's position.

They all became *advocates* (n.) of his proposal, however, when the king's son threatened to behead them.

AESTHETIC adj. (ES-THET-TIC) concerned with or appreciative of beauty

The queen, with her fine, *aesthetic* sense, decided to stage the abdication with an eye towards high drama and bright colors.

The queen considered her lady-in-waiting a true *aesthete* (n.) and often consulted with her when it came to matters of beauty and taste.

AFFINITY n. sympathy, attraction, kinship

She possessed an *affinity* for the local artists, so she called upon them to display their wares at a pre-abdication crafts fair.

AGENDA n. program, things to be done

The queen's *agenda* grew longer every day and was impossible to address.

AGGRANDIZE v. to make great

The king's wealth had *aggrandized* (v.) during the time of his reign.

The queen had also experienced an *aggrandizement* (n.) of her wealth.

ALLUSION n. (A-LOO-ZHUN) an indirect reference

She was sometimes referred to as Queen Jackie, which was an *allusion* to Jacqueline Onassis and her famous shopping sprees.

ALTRUISTIC adj. (AL-TROO-IS-TIC) unselfish concern with the welfare of others

The royal family, despite their excesses, had been quite *altruistic* about the fairness of the tax system.

AMNESTY n. an official pardon for a group of people who violate a law

In fact, the king himself had granted *amnesty* five years before to a ring of conspirators who had been planning to rob a bank.

⚡ANIMOSITY n. ill will, active dislike

He harbored no *animosity* towards the conspirators, even though a portion of his own money rested in the bank's vaults.

⚡ANOMALOUS adj. (A-NOM-A-LUS) irregular, abnormal, unusual

The prince secretly plans to hang all criminals once he is crowned, as he considers his father's decision regarding amnesty an *anomalous* one.

🚦 Plug In

Plug in your answers to see if you've got the right word power connections. For this quiz, circle the correct definition.

1. ABRIDGE
    (a) to cross
    (b) to build
    (c) to shorten

2. ABDICATE
    (a) to rush toward
    (b) to step up
    (c) to relinquish power

3. ABYSMAL
    (a) sickly
    (b) wretched
    (c) dark and dank

4. ANOMALOUS
    (a) interesting
    (b) unattractive
    (c) irregular

5. ABSOLVE
    (a) to forgive
    (b) to argue
    (c) to inspire

6. ACQUIESCE
   (a) to approve
   (b) to inherit
   (c) to give in

7. ADVOCATE
   (a) to punish
   (b) to support
   (c) to disdain

8. AFFINITY
   (a) hatred
   (b) familiarity
   (c) indecision

9. AGENDA
   (a) diary
   (b) schedule
   (c) reference book

10. ALLUSION
    (a) reference
    (b) trick
    (c) saying

11. ALTRUISTIC
    (a) truthful
    (b) generous
    (c) secretive

12. AMNESTY
    (a) affection
    (b) gift
    (c) pardon

13. AGGRANDIZEMENT
    (a) flattery
    (b) growth
    (c) pleasure

14. AESTHETIC
    - (a) sense of beauty
    - (b) joy of freedom
    - (c) joy of life

15. ANIMOSITY
    - (a) love
    - (b) dislike
    - (c) attraction for

⫶Recharge

Here are the answers to the Plug In quiz. Check to see if you made the right connections! Test yourself again on the words and definitions you missed.

1. c	6. c	11. b
2. c	7. b	12. c
3. b	8. b	13. b
4. c	9. b	14. a
5. a	10. a	15. b

Climb Every Mountain

⚡ARDUOUS adj. difficult to do, laborious

Sam knew the mountain-climbing expedition would be *arduous*.

Jenna, Sam's wife, having experienced the *arduousness* (n.) of the last climb, decided not to go.

⚡AUGMENT v. to increase or enlarge

Sam felt it important to *augment* the number of guides he employed for the climb.

⚡AUSTERE adj. (AWE-STEER) stern in manner or appearance, strict in morals

He also felt that the group should follow an *austere* routine, as any frivolity could cost them lives.

News of this *austerity* (n.) disillusioned many potential climbers, and many started to back out of the trip.

⚡AVERSION n. strong or fixed dislike, a feeling of repugnance

Sam had a decided *aversion* to joy seekers anyway, because they usually wasted too much of his time.

⚡ BANAL adj. (BUH-NAL) commonplace, trite, unoriginal

He particularly hated climbers like Harrison who, with his fancy airs and fancier equipment, struck him as utterly *banal.*

The *banality* (n.) of his countenance struck the other climbers as merely humorous.

BAROQUE adj. (BUH-ROKE) extravagantly ornate, flamboyant, characterized by bold ornamentation

Harrison's wife, Diana, who favored brocade gowns and velvet wraps studded with jewels, decided not to climb in favor of shopping for other *baroque* accoutrements.

BEGRUDGE v. to envy another's possessions, to concede reluctantly

Harrison did not usually *begrudge* Diana her purchases, but this time he did feel slightly annoyed.

BENEDICTION n. a blessing, a good wish

He would have considered her company on this climb a *benediction.*

BENIGN adj. (BUH-NINE) gentle, not harmful, kind

Diana, however, viewed her refusal as completely *benign,* because Harrison was well aware that climbing did not suit her.

BLANCH v. to turn pale

So it was no surprise that she *blanched* when Harrison lit into her.

BLITHE adj. (BLYTHE) happily, lighthearted, joyful

She had *blithely* (adv.) assumed Harrison wouldn't care.

Her *blithe* attitude often got Diana in trouble, as most people took life far more seriously.

BOTCH v. to bungle, to foul up

> "Darling!" she exclaimed, "I certainly *botched* this up, didn't I?"

BRACING adj. invigorating; v. to prepare

> "We must *brace* (v.) ourselves for a difficult separation," Harrison replied sternly.

> "All right," Diana nodded, "But first let's go for a *bracing* walk in the cold air."

BROACH v. to open up a subject for discussion

> Harrison hoped Diana would not attempt to *broach* a conversation about his hurt feelings.

BUFFOON n. clown or fool

> Harrison hated talking about his feelings with anyone but Sam's wife Jenna . . . a fact that made him feel like a tremendous *buffoon*.

Plug In

Plug in your answers to see if you've made the right word power connections. Fill in the blank by each word, matching it to its correct definition.

___	1. AUSTERE	(a)	reluctantly allow
___	2. ARDUOUS	(b)	a blessing
___	3. BANAL	(c)	harmless
___	4. BAROQUE	(d)	turn pale
___	5. BLITHE	(e)	make bigger
___	6. AUGMENT	(f)	invigorating
___	7. BEGRUDGE	(g)	bring up in conversation
___	8. BENEDICTION	(h)	difficult
___	9. BLANCH	(i)	elaborately fancy
___	10. BENIGN	(j)	trite
___	11. AVERSION	(k)	fool
___	12. BUFFOON	(l)	strict
___	13. BROACH	(m)	happy
___	14. BOTCH	(n)	ruin
___	15. BRACING	(o)	dislike

☀️*Recharge*

Here are the answers to the Plug In quiz. Check to see if you made the right connections! Test yourself again on the ones you missed.

1.	l	6.	e	11.	o
2.	h	7.	a	12.	k
3.	j	8.	b	13.	g
4.	i	9.	d	14.	n
5.	m	10.	c	15.	f

lesson 3

Peaceniks

BULWARK n. something used as a defense, a strong protection

The villagers used dirt and logs to provide a *bulwark* against the army's invading tanks.

CACHE n. (CASH) a hiding place, something hidden in a secret place

The guerrillas had a weapons *cache* in an underground tunnel.

CALLOUS adj. (CAL-LUS) unfeeling and insensitive

The army officers were *callous* about the destruction of the villages.

CANDOR adj. truthfulness, great honesty, frankness

The villagers tried to communicate with complete *candor.*

CAPITULATE v. to surrender, to stop resisting

The army would not *capitulate,* even in the face of increasing violent resistance.

CATHARSIS n. an emotional purification, an emotional release

It was a *catharsis* for the army soldiers when they heard the rescue helicopters.

They had a *cathartic* (adj.) experience viewing the tragedy on the stage.

CAUSTIC adj. (CAW-STICK) biting in humor

News traveled fast, and the usually witty General Quarters could not even muster a *caustic* remark.

CENSURE n. (SEN-SHUR) the act of blaming or condemning

He did, however, issue an angry *censure* against the guerrillas.

He *censured* (v.) them for their brutality.

CHASTISE v. to criticize severely

The guerrillas, though *chastised*, had no regrets.

The *chastisement* (n.) made them angrier, as it seemed to indicate the army had learned nothing.

CHRONIC adj. (KRON-ICK) constant, lasting a long time

The villagers hoped their conflicts with the army would not be *chronic*.

CIRCUMSPECT adj. careful, thought through

The battle had made Lieutenant Louis, one of the few survivors, more *circumspect* when facing his enemy.

He greeted each potential confrontation with increased *circumspection* (n.).

CLEMENCY n. disposition towards mercy, mildness

Lieutenant Louis even looked upon his own men with a gentler eye, granting *clemency* to a few privates who'd been caught stealing.

CLIQUE n. (KLEEK) an exclusive group

Among the privates a *clique* began to grow, devoting itself to honoring the villagers' perspective.

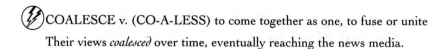

COALESCE v. (CO-A-LESS) to come together as one, to fuse or unite

Their views *coalesced* over time, eventually reaching the news media.

COHERENT adj. (CO-HERE-ENT) making sense, organized and logical

The privates finally decided to write down their views in a *coherent* manifesto that they hoped would bring global attention to the region and end the fighting.

Plug In

Plug in your answers to see if you've the right word power connections. Finish the sentences below, using the words below.

(a) bulwark   (f) catharsis   (k) circumspect

(b) cache   (g) caustic   (l) clemency

(c) callous   (h) censure   (m) clique

(d) candor   (i) chastise   (n) coalesce

(e) capitulate   (j) chronic   (o) coherent

1. Molly hid her _____ of antique dolls behind the staircase.

2. Jamal had a _____ habit of sneezing when he got nervous.

3. The sheriff granted _____ to the robbers because he was drunk.

4. It was a major _____ when Jill finally told Kevin off.

5. The sixth grade _____ was notorious for insensitive behavior.

6. The flu shot is a _____ against infection.

7. Julie was _____ for her fiendish public remarks about her old boyfriend.

8. Mr. Doty managed to write a _____ eulogy for his partner, but he couldn't read it.

9. "You are so _____ !" Beth declared when her boyfriend criticized her handling of a personal crisis.

10. The results from the score of experiments finally began to _____ in the scientist's mind.

11. Mrs. Antonioni _____ her son for being rude.

12. Jeremy remained _____ even after his partner was finished speaking, as he needed private time to consider the facts.

13. Professor Green spoke with total _____ when he informed his class that no one deserved anything better than a C on the midterm.

14. Adriana would not _____, even when informed that if she did not get dressed there would be no dessert for a week.

15. Anthony, smiling bitterly, became _____ when the woman he intended to marry threatened to return the ring.

☀️ Recharge

Here are the answers to this quiz. Check to see if you made the right word power connections! Plug in again and test yourself on the ones you missed.

1.	b	6.	a	11.	i
2.	j	7.	h	12.	k
3.	l	8.	o	13.	d
4.	f	9.	c	14.	e
5.	m	10.	n	15.	g

Love Me, Love My Writing

COLLOQUIAL adj. (COL-O-KWEE-UL) conversational, used in informal speech

The book was written in a *colloquial* style so that the information would be more user-friendly.

COMPATIBLE adj. able to get along well

The author was quite *compatible* with her editor; they communicated well.

CONVEY v. to transport, to conduct, to communicate

It is sometimes difficult to *convey* to an author the sort of revisions that are needed on a manuscript.

CONVICTION n. determination, a state of being convinced

Often an author cannot see the need for any changes and announces with *conviction* that the manuscript is perfection.

COPIOUS adj. abundant, lavish

Authors much prefer *copious* praise for their work to any other type of response.

CORROBORATE v. to support with evidence

If they don't receive flattery from their editors, authors have been known to seek out others who will *corroborate* their abilities.

This *corroboration* (n.) however, will usually not change an editor's mind.

CRAVEN adj. cowardly

It was the editor's *craven* decision to write out his criticisms on paper the day before taking a vacation.

CRITERION n. (CRY-TEER-EE-ON) standard for judging (plural: CRITERIA)

The *criterion* for determining the strength of a manuscript varies from editor to editor, and often depends on what book buyers are purchasing.

CURSORY adj. brief, without much attention to detail

The author gave the editor's letter a *cursory* look and, without even finishing it, promptly decided to call her agent.

DEARTH adj. (DURTH) a shortage

"Don't worry," the agent chuckled. "There is a *dearth* of material on this subject. You two will work it out."

DEFERENCE n. respect, courtesy

The author, in *deference* to her agent, went back to reread the editor's letter suggesting numerous revisions.

DEFT adj. skillful

She had to admit the editor was *deft* at phrasing a criticism in a positive light.

The editor *deftly* (adv.) critiqued the work with honesty and sensitivity.

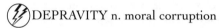DELINEATE v. to describe or picture in words, to detail

The necessary revisions were clearly *delineated*, leaving no room for confusion or misunderstanding.

DELUDE v. to deceive; to have false illusions

The author decided it was best not to *delude* herself into thinking the manuscript needed few changes, because in fact, the editor was right. It needed quite a bit of work.

DEPRAVITY n. moral corruption

Besides, the topic of the book was the moral *depravity* in many of today's art forms, and the author felt honor bound to follow her conscience.

🚦 Plug In

Plug in your answers to see if you've made the right word power connections. Circle *correct* or *incorrect* for the usage of each italicized word in the following sentences.

1. Jamika, a graduate of Oxford, writes in a formal, *colloquial* way.
   CORRECT   INCORRECT

2. Derek hit the table with frustration and exclaimed, "We are so *compatible*. We can't agree on a thing."
   CORRECT   INCORRECT

3. The truck was used to *convey* the goods to another store.
   CORRECT   INCORRECT

4. Dana sighed with *conviction* — she simple couldn't decide what to do.
   CORRECT   INCORRECT

5. The fruit was *copious*, but she wanted none of the mound before her.
   CORRECT   INCORRECT

6. Paul could truthfully *corroborate* Jim's telling of the story, as he knew nothing.
   CORRECT   INCORRECT

7. Melissa's refusal to support her friend in the face of a false accusation was a *craven* act.

CORRECT   INCORRECT

8. The *criterion* for a passing grade is the clear command of dates and names.

CORRECT   INCORRECT

9. Mrs. Lapinsky gave the recipe a *cursory* read and, after memorizing every last detail, she walked into the kitchen.

CORRECT   INCORRECT

10. Nudge was thrilled with the *dearth* of jewels in her possession as she had always loved to drape herself in diamonds and rubies.

CORRECT   INCORRECT

11. Out of *deference* to her Uncle, Patti did not invite his ex-wife to her wedding.

CORRECT   INCORRECT

12. Michael was *deft* at fencing, and so he switched to a sport he could conquer more easily.

CORRECT   INCORRECT

13. Mark *delineated* in his proposal the specific goals of the new business plan.

CORRECT   INCORRECT

14. Jenny refused to *delude* herself into thinking she would be the next Barbra Streisand.

CORRECT   INCORRECT

15. The seasoned pirates behaved with such *depravity* that even the most loyal of young ship hands had to turn away.

CORRECT   INCORRECT

The answer key appears on the following page.

🔆 *Recharge*

Here are the answers to the Plug In quiz. Check to see if you made the right connections!

1. incorrect—*colloquial* is informal
2. incorrect—*compatible* would mean they agree
3. correct
4. incorrect—*conviction* would mean she could decide
5. correct
6. incorrect—one can't *corroborate* something one doesn't know
7. correct
8. correct
9. incorrect—*cursory* would mean she only glanced at the recipe
10. incorrect—*dearth* would mean she had very little jewelry
11. correct
12. incorrect—*deft* would mean he was skillful at fencing
13. correct
14. correct
15. correct

Was She a Diva or a Dupe?

DEPRECIATE v. (DE-PREE-SHE-ATE) to lessen in value, to belittle

The extravagant car Janet wished to buy would, she knew, *depreciate* in value.

DESECRATE v. to treat with disrespect

"Do not *desecrate* your grandmother's memory with such a frivilous purchase," her father warned.

Janet had inherited a small fortune from her grandmother, and he felt it would be a *desecration* (n.) of her memory to spend it so foolishly.

DESTITUTE adj. very poor, totally lacking

He also warned Janet that if she didn't watch her money more carefully, she would one day be *destitute*.

"You are headed for *destitution* (n.)!" he cried.

DIATRIBE n. (DIE-A-TRIBE) a denunication, a biting speech

When Janet refused to take her father seriously, he flew into a lengthy *diatribe* about hard work and saving—and how she does neither.

DIDACTIC adj. instructive, intended to educate

Janet's father was also rather *didactic*, instructing her on how to go about putting money away for the lean times.

(⚡)DIFFUSE adj. wordy, not concentrated; v. to spread widely

His speech grew more and more *diffuse* (adj.) and impassioned.

Unrelated thoughts diffused (v.) his rantings, and Janet grew irritated.

DIGRESS v. to stray from the main subject

He *digressed* (v.) so often that Janet wasn't sure what he was getting at.

The *digressions* (n.) became rather colorful.

(⚡)DISCERNING adj. (DIS-EARNING) keenly perceptive, shrewd

Janet suddenly remembered that her father was quite *discerning* about his loved ones, revealing in his words a deep understanding of each person's weaknesses.

DISCOUNT v. to deduct, to disregard

Janet, in fact, found it harder and harder to *discount* his ideas, and she began to worry about the car.

DIVA n. (DEE-VA) an opera singer, prima donna; a tempermental, conceited person

She began to wonder if she was acting like a *diva* in her desire for the fancy car.

DOCILE adj. (DOS-EYEL) easily taught, submissive

Janet grew so lost in thought that she appeared quite *docile* as her father grew more and more emotional.

He mistook her apparant *docility* (n.) for acquiescence.

(⚡)DOGMATIC adj. arrogantly assertive, positive about unproven ideas

"If you buy the car, you will go broke," he said in his typically *dogmatic* style.

DORMANT adj. as though asleep, not actively growing

At that moment, all of Janet's resentment, which had been dormant, suddenly rose up in a fury.

DUPE v. (DOOP) to deceive, to trick

"I will not be *duped* into fearing for my future simply because I want something you can't appreciate!" she shrieked.

I will not be his little *dupe* (n.), she thought.

EBB v. to decline, to recede

Having expressed her anger so directly, Janet felt the rage begin to *ebb*, and so she said she'd give him a ride just as soon as the car was in her posession.

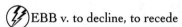Plug In

Plug in your answers to see if you've made the right word power connections. Do you have the power? Fill in the blank by each word, matching it to its correct definition.

__ 1. DEPRECIATE	(a) easily taught
__ 2. DESECRATE	(b) prima donna
__ 3. DESTITUTE	(c) to disregard
__ 4. DIATRIBE	(d) keenly perceptive
__ 5. DIDACTIC	(e) extremely poor
__ 6. DIFFUSE	(f) stray from main subject
__ 7. DIGRESS	(g) arrogantly assertive
__ 8. DISCERNING	(h) in a resting state
__ 9. DISCOUNT	(i) to flow back
__ 10. DIVA	(j) to deceive
__ 11. DOCILE	(k) to spread out
__ 12. DOGMATIC	(l) bitter speech
__ 13. DORMANT	(m) to treat with disrespect
__ 14. DUPE	(n) to lessen in value
__ 15. EBB	(o) positive in matters of opinion

⌖Recharge

Here are the answers to this quiz. Check to see if you made the right connections! Test yourself again on the ones you missed.

1.	n	6.	k	11.	a
2.	m	7.	f	12.	g
3.	e	8.	d	13.	h
4.	l	9.	c	14.	j
5.	o	10.	b	15.	i

lesson 6

Eric the Eccentric

ECCENTRIC adj. (EK-SEN-TRIK) nonconventional, a little kooky

Eric had such *eccentric* taste in hats that people would often smile as he passed.

Actually his *eccentricity* (n.) extended beyond the hats—he was famous for his odd behavior.

ECLECTIC adj. (EK-KLEC-TIC) drawn from many sources

Eric's taste in art, however, was *eclectic,* as he had equal passion for Picasso, Rembrandt, and Frida Kahlo.

EFFACE v. (EE-FACE) to erase, to rub away the features, to obscure

The truth was, Eric wished to efface the details of his past by creating a new, highly entertaining persona.

EGOCENTRIC adj. (EE-GO-SEN-TRIK) self-involved, selfish

Eric was quite *egocentric* in that he concerned himself very little with the needs of his friends.

They, in turn, were used to his *egocentricity* (n.) and grew to expect relatively little generosity and compassion from him.

EGREGIOUS adj. (UH-GREE-JUS) extremely bad, flagrant

It was only when Eric behaved in an *egregious* fashion, such as the time he laughed at his friend's broken leg, that any one of them mentioned his narcissism.

ELUCIDATE v. (E-LOO-SI-DATE) to make clear

Eric was so unaware of his own insensitivity that it was often necessary for his friends to *elucidate* the reasons for their annoyance and hurt.

EMBELLISH v. to add to, to exaggerate, garnish, ornament

Eric would listen with shock and then offer all kinds of excuses for his behavior, *embellishing* his points with woeful tales of a traumatic childhood.

No one was impressed with his lame *embellishments* (n.).

EMIGRATE v. to move to a new country, to move to a new place

Eric sulked and spoke of *emigrating* to the "old country" where he would be more appreciated.

His friends would patiently explain that his *emigration* (n.) would make them quite sad.

EMISSARY n. a messenger or representative, an agent

Eric would ignore their protests and dramatically announce that because of his great facility with the English language, he could become an *emissary* for his native land.

EMULATE v. to imitate, to strive to equal

His friends suspected he dreamed of *emulating* James Bond, but Eric would have made a lousy spy.

ENGAGING adj. charming, interesting

Eric was quite sure he was as *engaging* as Ian Fleming's secret agent, though perhaps not quite as handsome.

ENIGMA n. a puzzle, a baffling situation, something obscure

Eric fancied his mysterious past as an *enigma* because he took great care in behaving in unpredictable ways and telling contradictory stories.

His friends did not find him nearly as *enigmatic* (adj.) as he had hoped they would.

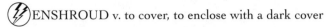

*⚡*ENSHROUD v. to cover, to enclose with a dark cover

Eric had one perplexing habit of *enshrouding* himself in black cloth every Friday night at ten minutes to midnight.

*⚡*ESOTERIC adj. understood by only a few

Eric assured his friends that this was an *esoteric* ritual he learned from an Indian mystic.

*⚡*EULOGIZE v. (YOU-LO-JIZE) to speak in praise of someone, to pay written or spoken tribute

"When I die," he told his friends, "You can all *eulogize* me. Tell everyone what a fantastic fellow I was!"

None of his friends, however, planned to give Eric the Eccentric such a *eulogy* (n.).

🔌 Plug In

Plug in your answers to see if you've made the right word power connections. Circle the correct definition for the following words.

1. ECCENTRIC
    (a) attractive
    (b) selfish
    (c) quirky

2. ECLECTIC
    (a) interesting
    (b) of varied sources
    (c) hard to grasp

3. EFFACE
    (a) to annoy
    (b) to insist
    (c) to erase

4. EGOCENTRIC
    (a) insensitive
    (b) terrible
    (c) self-centered

5. EGREGIOUS
   (a) creative
   (b) unclear
   (c) very bad

6. ELUCIDATE
   (a) to make clear
   (b) to give in
   (c) to cover

7. EMBELLISH
   (a) to adorn
   (b) to abbreviate
   (c) to prosper

8. EMIGRATE
   (a) to admonish
   (b) to repeat
   (c) to move

9. EMISSARY
   (a) a teacher
   (b) a message
   (c) a representative

10. EMULATE
    (a) to approve
    (b) to appreciate
    (c) to immitate

11. ENGAGING
    (a) popular
    (b) busy
    (c) charming

12. ENIGMA
    (a) a sign
    (b) a conflict
    (c) a puzzle

13. ENSHROUD
    (a) to cover
    (b) to worship
    (c) to inspire

14. ESOTERIC
    (a) lovely but unusual
    (b) profoundly artistic
    (c) understood by a few

15. EULOGIZE
    (a) to criticize
    (b) to amuse
    (c) to make tribute

·ᄋ·*Recharge*

Here are the answers to this quiz. Check to see if you made the right connections!

1. c	6. a	11. c
2. b	7. a	12. c
3. c	8. c	13. a
4. c	9. c	14. c
5. c	10. c	15. c

Send in the Clones

EXACERBATE v. (EX-AS-SIR-BATE) to make worse or more severe

Rosie *exacerbated* the situation by walking out during Donald's opening remarks.

EXACTING adj. greatly demanding, requiring close attention

They had argued earlier over his *exacting* approach to the speech which she had said should be delivered in a more delicate, careful fashion.

EXALT v. to raise high, to glorify

Donald had started off as a lab technician before his boss decided to *exalt* him by allowing him to head up the cloning experiment.

Donald was successful and he was promptly promoted to what he felt was an *exalted* (adj.) position.

EXORBITANT adj. extravagant, exceeding what is usual

Still, Donald had a fragile ego and was in need of *exorbitant* praise, in particular, from Rosie.

EXPEDITE v. to make faster or easier, to carry out promptly

He would often try to *expedite* matters by leaving notes around the lab (in duplicate!) with compliments she might think of extending to him.

Rosie did not consider this an *expeditious* (adj.) plan as she had no intention of following a script.

EXPLICIT adj. (EX-PLI-SIT) clearly stated, precisely shown

Rosie gave *explicit* reasons for her reluctance to flatter Donald, including the fact that he never thought to flatter her.

EXPUNGE v. to erase, to strike out

Ignoring her complaint, Donald told Rosie, "You would have me *expunge* the cloning details from my speech in favor of a less scientific talk!"

EXTOL v. to praise highly

"That is a decision I could *extol*," Rosie remarked dryly.

FACADE n. (FA-SOD) the principal front of a building, a false appearance

"You have a *facade* of such warmth and understanding, but actually Rosie, you're very cold," Donald complained bitterly.

FACTION n. a group, or part of a large group, united on an issue

Rosie sighed. "You boob," she told him. "There is a *faction* in the audience that believes your experiments are immoral. You need to be more cautious."

FALLACY n. (FAL-A-SEE) false idea, mistaken belief, an implausible argument

Donald's belief that the audience would be swayed by his scientific expertise was, she knew, a *fallacy*.

His findings were not *fallacious* (adj.), but the audience would be mistrustful.

FAWNING v. to show excessive affection, to be overly flattering in return for favor

Many of Donald's lab assistants had been *fawning* all over him, making it difficult for him to see the truly controversial side of cloning.

FEIGN v. (FANE) to pretend, give a false impression, to invent falsely

The audience *feigned* total support for Donald, but Rosie knew they were stirring up trouble behind his back.

FIDELITY n. a state of being faithful, loyal

"My *fidelity* to cloning may be blinding me to some problems," Donald sheepishly admitted.

FINESSE v. (FIN-ESS) delicacy of workmanship, subtlety, skillful maneuvering

Donald decided to *finesse* his cloning speech so that his detractors could not attack it. "Double your pleasure," he began, "double your fun."

Plug In

Plug in your answers to see if you've made the right word power connections.

1. The ointment exacerbated Jeanette's cut so that it healed more quickly.
    CORRECT   INCORRECT

2. Mrs. Klein's analysis of the situation was so exacting that her own daughter accused her of not caring one bit.
    CORRECT   INCORRECT

3. Principal Lussier felt exalted by his nomination to the newly funded Council on Education.
    CORRECT   INCORRECT

4. The price for a basket of berries was so exorbitant that Molly bought ten to give as gifts.
    CORRECT   INCORRECT

5. To expedite her speedy escape from the office, Juanita refused to answer her phone.
    CORRECT   INCORRECT

6. Jane's description of her romantic evening with Barry was so explicit, even her best friend felt embarrassed.
    CORRECT   INCORRECT

7. Zac expunged all mention of his relationship with Judy from his diary, in the hope of forgetting her.
    CORRECT   INCORRECT

8. Leon extolled the beauty of his new girlfriend, but said nothing of her questionable intelligence.
   CORRECT　　　　　　INCORRECT

9. Sean could not figure out how someone with such a lovely facade could always looks so angry and unfriendly.
   CORRECT　　　　　　INCORRECT

10. The girls read the faction quite carefully, but could not understand a word of it.
    CORRECT　　　　　　INCORRECT

11. Richard's belief that his son could one day play college basketball was truly a fallacy, as his son, at age eight, could already play as well as some thirteen-year-olds.
    CORRECT　　　　　　INCORRECT

12. Patricia's mother fawned over her to such a degree that the flattery even sickened Patricia.
    CORRECT　　　　　　INCORRECT

13. Jesse feigned sickness rather than attend her piano recital.
    CORRECT　　　　　　INCORRECT

14. "I have had it," Walter exclaimed. "Never again. And that's fidelity!"
    CORRECT　　　　　　INCORRECT

15. Steve, tripping twice and falling once, finessed the figure skating program.
    CORRECT　　　　　　INCORRECT

☼ *Recharge*

Here are the answers to this quiz. Check to see if you made the right connections! Test yourself again in a week on the ones you missed.

1.	incorrect	6.	correct	11.	correct
2.	incorrect	7.	correct	12.	correct
3.	correct	8.	correct	13.	correct
4.	incorrect	9.	incorrect	14.	incorrect
5.	correct	10.	incorrect	15.	incorrect

Her Lucky Break

FLEDGLING n. a young bird learning to fly; a beginner, a novice

Gina was clearly a *fledgling* performer.

FLOURISH v. (FLUR-ISH) to grow strong, to grow abundantly, to thrive or prosper; to make broad and sweeping gestures

She was bound to *flourish*, however, under the tutelage of Maestro Maurice.

He was known for the way in which he *flourished* his baton.

FLUKE n. a chance event, a coincidence, a stroke of luck

The Maestro's discovery of Gina was a *fluke*.

FODDER n. raw material for a given end

In fact, the story was *fodder* for many a musical gossip column.

FORAY n. an initial venture, to raid in search of plunder

Gina's first *foray* onto the stage was something of a disaster.

The reviewers had gone on a *foray* to pillory fledgling performers.

FORFEIT v. (FOR-FIT) to give up something as a penalty for some error or crime

Gina was forced to *forfeit* her right to play the antique Steinway because she kept arriving late for practices.

This *forfeiture* (n.) cost her a fine performance.

⚡ FORTUITOUS adj. (FOR-TOO-I-TUS) happening by chance; lucky or fortunate

Nothing in Gina's life had ever been *fortuitous*, and this incident was typical.

Her fortunes changed when she was able to play the beloved Steinway and Maestro Maurice *fortuitously* (adv.) happened by.

⚡ FURTIVE adj. secret, done by stealth, sly

The Maestro was *furtive* in his attentions to Gina, making it seem as if he were studying his score rather than listening to her.

He *furtively* (adv.) looked up now and then to study the young pianist.

⚡ FUTILE adj. (FEW-TILE) useless, hopeless, without effect

Gina, knowing this would not be the piano she could use in her performance, imagined her practice session was *futile* in terms of developing her career.

⚡ GALVANIZE v. to arouse suddenly, to stimulate, spur to action

Suddenly, however, she was aware of the Maestro's presence, and she became *galvanized*.

GAMUT n. the full range of something

Her playing ran through the gamut of emotions, reaching depths she hardly knew she possessed.

⚡ GARNER v. to gather and store away, to acquire by effort

Gina attempted to *garner* every inch of Maestro Maurice's attention by playing as if her life depended on the excellence of her performance.

GENTEEL adj. (JEN-TEEL) refined, polite, aristocratic

In the past, she'd been accused of playing in a too *genteel* style.

Gina left her *gentility* (n.) behind as she plunged into her performance.

GRATUITOUS adj. (GRA-TOO-I-TUS) freely given, unnecessary, uncalled for, unwarranted

When Gina was almost finished, Maestro Maurice walked away, leaving Gina to wonder if even a *gratuitous* remark would have been better than this obvious snub.

GRAVITY adj. seriousness

The *gravity* of the situation was soon forgotten when the Maestro returned with a bouquet of flowers and personally invited Gina to study with him.

Plug In

Plug in your answers to see if you've made the right word power connections. Choose the correct definition for the following words.

1. FLEDGLING
   - (a) a chance event
   - (b) a novice
   - (c) a venture

2. FLOURISH
   - (a) to feel hopeless
   - (b) to hide
   - (c) to grow

3. FLUKE
   - (a) a lucky break
   - (b) a secret
   - (c) a full range

4. FODDER
   - (a) raw material
   - (b) luck
   - (c) unnecessary

5. FORAY
   - (a) to walk with stealth
   - (b) to grow well
   - (c) to venture forth

6. FORFEIT
   (a) to pay a penalty
   (b) to plunder
   (c) to lose hope

7. FORTUITOUS
   (a) well deserved
   (b) without effect
   (c) a chance occurrence

8. FURTIVE
   (a) secret
   (b) clumsily
   (c) serious

9. FUTILE
   (a) a lucky break
   (b) a coincidence
   (c) hopeless

10. GALVANIZE
    (a) to inspire
    (b) to stimulate
    (c) to insult

11. GAMUT
    (a) a mistake
    (b) an insult
    (c) a range

12. GARNER
    (a) to impress
    (b) to appreciate
    (c) to gather

13. GENTEEL
    (a) earthy
    (b) gentle
    (c) polite

14. GRATUITOUS
    (a) important
    (b) desirable
    (c) unnecessary

15. GRAVITY
    (a) graciousness
    (b) great
    (c) seriousness

☀ *Recharge*

Here are the answers to this quiz. Check to see if you made the right word power connections! Test yourself again on the ones you missed.

1. b	6. a	11. c
2. c	7. c	12. c
3. a	8. a	13. c
4. a	9. c	14. c
5. c	10. b	15. c

Slumming It

GRIMACE v. to make an ugly disapproving facial expression

Gregory *grimaced* when he first walked into his future apartment.

GROVEL v. to beg persistently, to degrade oneself

He had *groveled* at the super's door hoping for an apartment—but he never imagined it would be this dirty!

GUILE n. cunning duplicity, purposeful deceit

Gregory had used no small amount of *guile* to secure himself the apartment, even claiming to be a war veteran.

GUISE n. an external appearance

This *guise* seemed to strike an emotional chord with the super.

GULLIBLE adj. easily deceived

The super had proven to be quite *gullible* and had practically cried when Gregory described his war wounds.

HARBINGER n. a precursor, an indication, one that foreshadows what is coming

Had Gregory been less intent on his mission, he might have taken as a *harbinger* the irate tenant who interrupted their chat to complain about "damp walls."

HERALD (v) to give notice of, to hail or greet

This interruption *heralded* the complaints of many other tenants.

But this first tenant was the *herald* (n.) of things to come.

HERESY n. any belief that is strongly opposed to established beliefs, or practice

Gregory was so grateful when the super granted him an apartment, he considered it *heresy* to even listen to another tenant's complaints.

HIATUS n. a break or interruption from work or any other established routine

In fact, he was so thrilled with the *hiatus* from apartment hunting, he sent the super tickets to an upcoming football game.

HOMAGE n. reverence, respect, an expression of high regard

Gregory, in effect, paid homage to a man who would eventually let him live in a veritable slum.

HOMOGENEOUS adj. similar, of the same kind, uniform in nature

The building had a rather *homogeneous* population, which Gregory thought might be a tad boring.

HUBRIS n. excessive pride, arrogance, exaggerated self-confidence

Gregory had the *hubris* to suggest to the super that in the future it might be wise to introduce tenants of different nationalities into the building.

HYPERBOLE n. (HI-PER-BUL-LEE) extravagant exaggeration used as a figure of speech

"This building could rival the United Nations!" Gregory exclaimed, using *hyperbole* to inspire the super.

IMMATERIAL adj. insignificant, unimportant

"Your suggestion is *immaterial* to me," the super replied quietly. "All I care about is tenants who pay up."

⚡ IMMINENT adj. about to occur, hanging threateningly over one's head

Gregory was disgruntled with this reply, unaware of the *imminent* disappointment and anger he was to experience upon viewing his disgustingly dirty new abode.

🚦 Plug In

Plug in your answers to see if you've made the right connections. Which sentences are correct?

1. Janet considered it an act of heresy when her sister lovingly decided to support Janet's decision.
       CORRECT   INCORRECT

2. The class was so homogeneous that every blue-eyed child looked alike.
       CORRECT   INCORRECT

3. James was given to using such extreme hyperbole that his teacher insisted he practice writing more expressively.
       CORRECT   INCORRECT

4. Tracy, completely without guile, managed to convince the teacher to give her an A, simply by virtue of her passion for the subject.
       CORRECT   INCORRECT

5. Jamal was so gullible that when his friend claimed there was a thief in the house, he simply ignored him.
       CORRECT   INCORRECT

6. Emily Jane took a hiatus from her job to venture down the Nile.
       CORRECT   INCORRECT

7. Andrea's hubris interfered with many a job interview as she was too shy to speak.
       CORRECT   INCORRECT

8. Musa was the harbinger of bad news during the strike because he was the only person the workers would address.
       CORRECT   INCORRECT

9. The prince paid homage to his father the king, though secretly he thought him incompetent and wished him dead.

    CORRECT   INCORRECT

10. Abdul found it immaterial that his new employee was incompetent with computers, since his entire business depended on a certain proficiency with computerized spreadsheets.

    CORRECT   INCORRECT

11. In her guise as a former child star, Mrs. Ricci was able to secure herself financial assistance from a theatrical charity.

    CORRECT   INCORRECT

12. Disaster was imminent, but the twins refused to abandon their home to the violent winds of a hurricane that threatened to strike at any moment.

    CORRECT   INCORRECT

13. The law forbidding the consumption of liquor heralded a very conservative era.

    CORRECT   INCORRECT

14. Rachel grimaced when she saw the glorious wedding gown—it was exactly what she'd hoped it would be.

    CORRECT   INCORRECT

15. Shannon groveled in front of the dean, promising never to cheat or steal again, but she was still expelled.

    CORRECT   INCORRECT

⚡ Recharge

Here are the answers to this quiz. Check to see if you made the right word power connections! Test yourself again on the ones you missed.

1.	incorrect	6.	correct	11.	correct
2.	correct	7.	incorrect	12.	correct
3.	correct	8.	correct	13.	correct
4.	correct	9.	correct	14.	incorrect
5.	incorrect	10.	incorrect	15.	correct

lesson 10

Justin Time

 IMMUTABLE adj. something that is unchangeable, permanent

It seemed as if poverty were an *immutable* fact of life for the Clifton family, as no Clifton ever had any money.

IMPERIOUS adj. commanding, lordly, arrogant

Justin Clifton, the youngest son, behaved in an *imperious* manner, most likely in an attempt to cover up his insecurities.

IMPOTENT adj. lacking power, helpless, unable to perform sexual intercourse

Jackson Clifton, the head of the family, wished he could change the dire circumstances, but felt *impotent* to do so. He had never graduated from high school.

INCESSANT adj. unceasing, neverending, flowing without interruption

Jackson's concerns were *incessant*, often keeping him up at night.

Patty Clifton, his wife, complained *incessantly* (adv.), but she couldn't find a job either.

INCIPIENT adj. beginning to be, in an early stage

The anger Justin felt was *incipient* and likely to grow stronger with the frustrations of each passing day.

INCONTROVERTIBLE adj. not disputable, not open to question

The fact that it would be extremely difficult and far too costly for Justin to attend college was *incontrovertible*.

INDIGENOUS adj. native, produced or living in a particular area

The Cliftons lived in a tiny shack surrounded by swamps and woods that were *indigenous* to the area.

⚡ INDIGENT adj. poverty stricken, needy

The *indigent* Cliftons were often hungry and cold.

Their *indigence* (n.) caught the eye of very few as their nearest neighbor was miles away.

⚡ INEPT adj. clumsy, awkward, incompetent

Jackson Clifton tried his hand at learning automotive repair, but his work was deemed *inept* by everyone in town.

His *ineptitude* (n.) resulted in two car accidents!

⚡ INFAMY n. an evil reputation borne of a criminal act, a reputation for evil deeds

Infamy came to the mayor of the Cliftons' town for his habit of pocketing bribes from local businesses.

He was already *infamous* (adj.) for a lack of interest in the poor.

INHIBIT v. to keep from free activity or expression, to restrain or even forbid

Jackson Clifton felt *inhibited* about approaching any more townsfolk for work.

His *inhibitions* (n.) stood in the way of his family's well-being.

INSIDIOUS adj. sly, treacherous, having a gradual effect

Jackson Clifton's fears and pride had an *insidious* effect on his family.

The *insidiousness* (n.) of the Clifton's problems left them confused and depressed, and Justin became terribly envious of anyone with money.

⚡ INSIPID adj. lacking taste, dull, bland

Yet every time Justin found himself sitting in school near Peter, the son of the town's attorney, he found the boy's conversation and humor *insipid*.

INTREPID adj. fearless, having fortitude and endurance

When Justin was in eighth grade, he became *intrepid* in his quest to

make a better life for himself.

IRREVERENT adj. disrespectful, gently or humorously mocking

When Justin grew up, he managed to become a banker by virtue of his intelligence, fortitude, and belated *irreverent* attitude about his youthful poverty.

His warm *irreverence* (n.) kept him laughing through life, opening the door to his success and the opportunity to help his grateful family.

░▓░ *Plug In*

Plug in your answers to see if you've made the right word power connections. Here's a twist—for each vocabulary word below, choose the word closest to the OPPOSITE meaning.

1. IMMUTABLE
   (a) beautiful
   (b) changeable
   (c) funny

2. IMPERIOUS
   (a) important
   (b) humble
   (c) prideful

3. IMPOTENT
   (a) forceful
   (b) impatient
   (c) powerless

4. INCESSANT
   (a) constant
   (b) occasional
   (c) annoying

5. INCIPIENT
   (a) mature
   (b) tasteless
   (c) native

6. INCONTROVERTIBLE
   (a) incoherent

(b) basic
(c) questionable

7. INDIGENOUS
   (a) poverty stricken
   (b) foreign
   (c) humorless

8. INDIGENT
   (a) wealthy
   (b) native
   (c) depressed

9. INEPT
   (a) possible
   (b) able
   (c) shy

10. INFAMY
    (a) glory
    (b) hatred
    (c) cruelty

11. INHIBIT
    (a) encourage
    (b) frustrate
    (c) insult

12. INSIDIOUS
    (a) growing
    (b) sudden
    (c) inexplicable

13. INSIPID
    (a) hateful
    (b) clever
    (c) depressed

14. INTREPID
    (a) capable
    (b) careful
    (c) deliberate

15. IRREVERENT
    (a) respectful
    (b) determined
    (c) insulting

⚡ *Recharge*

Here are the answers to this quiz. Check to see if you made the right word power connections! Test yourself again on the ones you missed.

1.	b	6.	c	11.	a
2.	b	7.	b	12.	b
3.	a	8.	a	13.	b
4.	b	9.	b	14.	b
5.	a	10.	a	15.	a

Everyone Knows It's Windy

JARGON n. a specialized vocabulary of a group, an obscure language

Brandon and Allison were so confused by the travel agent's *jargon* that they simply said, "Fine. Book the trip. The Isle of Fiero sounds okay."

JAUNT n. (JAWNT) a short pleasure trip

They had worked hard all year and were looking forward to a *jaunt* out of the country.

JEOPARDY n. (JEP-ER-DEE) exposure to danger, peril

It never occurred to Brandon or Allison that they could be in any sort of *jeopardy* on such a brief pleasure trip.

JUDICIOUS adj. (JOO-DISH-US) wise, showing judgment, cautious

As it turned out, their decision to go with the fast-talking agent's plan was not a *judicious* one.

JUNCTION n. a place of meeting or joining, a linkup

After their flight to the Isle of Fiero, Brandon and Allison took a taxi to the *junction* of Banana Street and Parrot Avenue to hire a tour guide.

JUXTAPOSE v. to place side by side

Allison *juxtaposed* the lovely tourist brochure photograph in her hand with the landscape visible through the taxi window, and she was bummed out — Fiero was hardly a tropical paradise.

KARMA n. a good or bad emanation of force from someone or something; in Hinduism and Buddhism the force created by someone's actions to perpetuate reincarnation

Allison was further disconcerted by the fear that their tour guide, Lucifer, had bad *karma*.

LACONIC adj. brief in speech, using very few words

Lucifer's *laconic* style left Allison frustrated and somewhat unnerved — and she didn't like his piercing eyes, either.

LAMENT v. to mourn, to express regret

"Honey, we should never have come here," Allison *lamented* to Brandon.

But her *lament* (n.) fell on deaf ears; Brandon was enthralled with Lucifer and the Isle of Fiero.

LATENT adj. present but not visible or apparent, dormant, potential

Allison's *latent* sense of danger began to emerge — her left eye started to twitch.

LAUD v. to praise, to applaud, to extol

With a sardonic smile, Lucifer started to *laud* Allison.

LAX adj. careless, too relaxed

"You are right to be afraid," Lucifer told Allison. "My guerrilla fighters have taken over Fiero and its *lax* government. We may decide to keep you both as prisoners."

LEGACY n. something handed down from the past, a bequest

Brandon's jaw dropped. "Is this the kind of violent *legacy* you want to pass on to your children?"

LEVITY n. lack of seriousness, frivolity

Lucifer's mood immediately changed. With great *levity* he said, "Oh, Sir, I was only joking! I think you and your wife need a vacation badly."

LIAISON n. (LEE-A-ZUN) connection between different groups, a close bond, an illicit sexual relationship

"But since we have developed a *liaison* with one another," Lucifer confided, "the latest weather report shows a hurricane will hit Fiero this evening. Didn't your travel agent warn you about our weather?"

Plug In

Plug in your answers to see if you've the right word power connections. Fill in the blank by each word, matching it to its correct definition.

__ 1. JAUNT	(a)	present, not visible
__ 2. JARGON	(b)	frivolity
__ 3. LAMENT	(c)	complain
__ 4. LACONIC	(d)	peril
__ 5. JEOPARDY	(e)	praise
__ 6. JUNCTION	(f)	too relaxed
__ 7. JUXTAPOSE	(g)	wise
__ 8. KARMA	(h)	personal force
__ 9. JUDICIOUS	(i)	a bequest
__ 10. LEVITY	(j)	a linkup
__ 11. LAX	(k)	place next to
__ 12. LEGACY	(l)	using few words
__ 13. LATENT	(m)	a close bond
__ 14. LAUD	(n)	a specialized language
__ 15. LIAISON	(o)	a brief trip

⌖ *Recharge*

Here are the answers to this quiz. Check to see if you made the right connections! Test yourself again on the ones you missed.

1.	o	6.	j	11.	f
2.	n	7.	k	12.	i
3.	c	8.	h	13.	a
4.	l	9.	g	14.	e
5.	d	10.	b	15.	m

Safari, So Good

LISTLESS adj. indifferent, a lack of energy, spiritless

Mariah often spent her days in a bathrobe, feeling utterly *listless*.

LUCID adj. clear, easily understood

When spoken to, she was quite *lucid*, but her eyes were sleepy and her manner, inattentive.

Her *lucidity* (n.) was unquestionable, but she always appeared bored and fatigued.

LUMINOUS adj. glowing, bright, emitting light

Mariah's sister Ali, however, had a *luminous* presence, charming everyone with her warmth and vitality.

Her *luminosity* (n.) was profound.

MAGNANIMOUS adj. noble in spirit, generous, giving

Ali was sweet to most people, but totally *magnanimous* when it came to Mariah.

Ali treated her sister *magnanimously* (adv.), forever trying to entertain and inspire her.

MALAISE n. a feeling of depression, uneasiness, of being unwell

Mariah often experienced a general *malaise* for days, no matter how Ali tried to buoy her spirits.

MANIFEST v. to make evident by showing

"Mariah," Ali said with great concern, "you are beginning to *manifest* some trouble symptoms. Please go see a doctor."

"It's just a *manifestation* (n.) of my diet, I think," said Mariah, listlessly. "I'll try to eat more leafy green vegetables."

MARSHAL v. to gather together something for a purpose, to arrange in order

Ali would often have to *marshal* all her patience when speaking to Mariah, but she felt it her duty to remain kind and involved.

MARTYR n. one who suffers for a cause, a person who sacrifices for a principle

It took a complete *martyr* to care for Mariah, and Ali fit the bill perfectly.

MAVERICK n. a person who breaks away from the crowd, a nonconformist

Ali's closest friend, Cleo, a true *maverick*, tried to convince Ali to leave Mariah for two weeks and go on a safari.

MEANDER v. to wander aimlessly

"Imagine *meandering* among the wild giraffe, lions, and hyenas!" said Cleo.

MERCENARY n. a person who serves only for money, motivated by greed

"Are you planning to hire a crazy *mercenary* to escort us on this jaunt, or do you think we can manage getting killed all on our own?" Ali joked.

"No one would be that *mercenary*," (adj.) Cleo replied.

MOOT adj. of no matter or consequence, not important

"Well, it's *moot* anyway," Ali sighed, "unless Mariah wants to join us."

MOROSE adj. gloomy, bad tempered, a sullen disposition

"Oh, please!" Cleo cried. "She's so *morose*, she wouldn't agree to a flight to Paris."

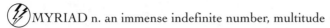

MYRIAD n. an immense indefinite number, multitude

"There are a *myriad* of things that excite Mariah," Ali shot back defensively, "though I confess I have yet to discover them all."

NEGLIGENT adj. careless, remiss

"Well, try being *negligent* with her for once, Ali. Mariah might be forced to discover life," Cleo suggested pointedly.

"You know," Ali said softly, "a bit of *negligence* (n.) and some African nights under the stars might do me a world of good . . . ."

Plug In

Plug in your answers to see if you've made the right word power connections. Choose the correct definition (or the word closest in meaning) for the following words.

1. LISTLESS
   (a) gloomy
   (b) indifferent
   (c) generous

2. LUCID
   (a) careless
   (b) visible
   (c) clear

3. MAGNANIMOUS
   (a) generous
   (b) immense
   (c) uneasy

4. MALAISE
   (a) greedy
   (b) sense of unwell
   (c) difficult

5. MANIFEST
   (a) apparent
   (b) not important
   (c) glow

6. NEGLIGENCE
   (a) temper
   (b) attention
   (c) carelessness

7. LUMINOUS
   (a) annoying
   (b) famous
   (c) shining bright

8. MARSHAL
   (a) gather
   (b) lead
   (c) fight

9. MARTYR
   (a) sufferer
   (b) angel
   (c) warrior

10. MAVERICK
    (a) a greedy person
    (b) a nonconformist
    (c) a lucky person

11. MYRIAD
    (a) a great number
    (b) a mystery
    (c) a sickness

12. MOOT
    (a) dumb
    (b) irrelevant
    (c) irrational

13. MEANDER
    (a) travel
    (b) wander
    (c) chase

14. MOROSE
    (a) frustrated
    (b) deadly
    (c) gloomy

15. MERCENARY
    (a) ambitious
    (b) greedy
    (c) daring

⚘·*Recharge*

Here are the answers to this quiz. Check to see if you made the right connections! Test yourself again on the ones you missed.

1. b	6. c	11. a
2. c	7. c	12. b
3. a	8. a	13. b
4. b	9. a	14. c
5. a	10. b	15. b

To Catch a Thief

NEMESIS n. a powerful rival, a usually unconquerable opponent

Nathaniel, the kingdom's only hope for law and order, had a formidable *nemesis*, the robber named Vardo.

NOMADIC adj. without a permanent home, constantly wandering

Vardo was difficult to track down as his *nomadic* lifestyle left a very scarce trail.

NOMINAL adj. insignificant, trifling

Nathaniel's efforts to capture Vardo were *nominal* concerns for the notorious thief.

Vardo was only *nominally* (adv.) shaken by Nathaniel's last attempt to bring him to justice.

NOVEL adj. new, original

Nathaniel decided he was going to have to use a *novel* approach to corner Vardo because his usual traps simply weren't working.

NUANCE n. (NOO-ANSE) a subtle distinction, a slight difference in definition

He wondered if it were simply a question of *nuance* rather than an entirely different approach to Vardo's capture.

NULLIFY v. to repeal, cancel, render void

Secretly, Nathaniel wished he could *nullify* the hostilities between them, but he would never say so out loud.

The *nullification* (n.) of their rivalry would have made his life easier.

⚡ OBLITERATE v. to blot out leaving no traces, to destroy

Vardo, on the other hand, enjoyed eluding capture, and he was happy that they hadn't managed to *obliterate* each other.

The *obliteration* (n.) of Nathaniel, in fact, would have depressed Vardo.

⚡ OBSCURE adj. unclear, vague partially hidden, hard to understand

Vardo kept his habits *obscure,* being careful not to establish many patterns that could lead to his arrest.

His *obscurity* (n.) contributed to his safety.

OBVIATE v. (OB-VEE-ATE) to make unnecessary, to avert, to preclude

Vardo's wandering lifestyle *obviated* the need for Nathaniel to uncover the method to his rival's madness. Only one thing promised to give Vardo away!

ODIOUS adj. (O-DEE-US) hateful, evil, vile

Vardo had an *odious* tendency to pull off a dramatic robbery, walk one mile in a northerly direction, and then sleep in a pigpen for three days.

ODYSSEY n. (ODD-UH-SEE) a long difficult journey marked by changes in fortune

Nathaniel reluctantly decided to undertake an *odyssey* to catch the thief.

⚡ OGLE v. (OG-UL) to stare at in a disrespectful way

Nathaniel dressed up as a milkmaid and journeyed to the site of Vardo's latest robbery. As he walked north of the crime scene, the peasants *ogled* him.

OLIGARCHY n. (O-LI-GAR-KEE) a government in which the power is in the hands of only a few

The kingdom was basically run as an *oligarchy,* and there was great unrest throughout the land.

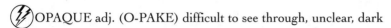

⚡OPAQUE adj. (O-PAKE) difficult to see through, unclear, dark

When Nathaniel spied Vardo asleep in a pigpen, he kept his expression *opaque* so as not to reveal his fears.

The *opacity* (n.) of his milkmaid's cloak made it impossible to see the armor he wore underneath.

⚡OPPORTUNIST n. a person who takes advantage of opportunity with no regard for principle

Vardo, being the ultimate *opportunist*, woke up, spied Nathaniel in disguise, hopped on the back of a giant hog, and trotted down the lane to safety.

Plug In

Plug in your answers to see if you've made the right word power connections. Which sentences are correct?

1. "You are my nemesis!" Sarina cried out, hugging her best friend.

    CORRECT   INCORRECT

2. Ben was happy with his nomadic lifestyle, and enjoyed periodically redecorating his home.

    CORRECT   INCORRECT

3. Ilze had the novel idea of replacing the knobs on her cabinets with little bells.

    CORRECT   INCORRECT

4. Darin was not one for nuance as he saw everything in very black and white terms.

    CORRECT   INCORRECT

5. "I hereby nullify taxation on books," the governor declared as book buyers across the state sighed with relief.

    CORRECT   INCORRECT

6. The bomb obliterated the entire village, but completely destroyed the open countryside.

    CORRECT   INCORRECT

7. Zoli's plans were so obscure that no one knew what she was going to do until she did it.

        CORRECT   INCORRECT

8. Maria's photographic memory obviated the need for her to memorize a thing.

        CORRECT   INCORRECT

9. There was an odious smell coming from the sink, so no one would enter the kitchen.

        CORRECT   INCORRECT

10. The dragonslayer undertook an odyssey to kill a deer for dinner that night.

        CORRECT   INCORRECT

11. The family ogled their neighbor's new Cadillac as they were much loved.

        CORRECT   INCORRECT

12. Mr. Robert Howard was head of the oligarchy, and he invited everyone's suggestions and comments.

        CORRECT   INCORRECT

13. "I will do the job for a nominal fee," said the artist, "but it may take a while to complete."

        CORRECT   INCORRECT

14. Rebecca selected opaque stockings because she was covered with bruises from rollerblading.

        CORRECT   INCORRECT

15. Tammy felt like an opportunist for answering the ad and promptly landing a job because she cared so much for the environment.

        CORRECT   INCORRECT

Recharge

Here are the answers to this quiz. Check to see if you made the right connections! Test yourself again on the ones you missed.

1.	incorrect	6.	incorrect	11.	incorrect
2.	incorrect	7.	correct	12.	incorrect
3.	correct	8.	correct	13.	correct
4.	correct	9.	correct	14.	correct
5.	correct	10.	incorrect	15.	incorrect

Drain, Baby, Drain!

OSMOSIS n. gradual or subtle absorption, an unconscious process of absorption

Pierre Pinnacle was so good at mastering languages that he seemed to learn them by *osmosis*.

OUST v. (OWST) to eject, to banish, to expel

Despite his linguistic prowess, his native principality of Swump threatened to *oust* him because of his unusual ideas.

OVERTURE n. an opening move, a preliminary offer

He had been making hostile *overtures* to other countries, but not one had given in to his demands.

PALATABLE adj. pleasant to the taste, agreeable in feeling

His belief that he alone should rule the world was simply not *palatable* to other governments.

PALTRY adj. (PAUL-TREE) a tiny or insignificant amount, meager, scant

Pierre Pinnacle thought he had made only *paltry* attempts to build a super weapon for global destruction, so why did everyone see him as a threatening figure?

PARIAH n. (PA-RYE-AH) an outcast

No one in Swump would talk with him, and he soon realized he was becoming a *pariah*. "Why is world domination driving my friends away?", Pierre Pinnacle wondered.

PARTITION n. a dividing wall, a division

He proposed to *partition* the world into two sections: one for his bird watching pleasure and the other for his sightseeing excursions.

PAUCITY n. (PAW-CITY) scarcity, smallness in number or amount

This idea was met with a *paucity* of enthusiasm, to say the least.

PEDANTIC adj. boringly scholarly, academic in mode

Pierre Pinnacle tried, in a *pedantic* manner, to explain why he was suited for the position of world ruler, but his rambling bored all listeners.

PENCHANT n. a strong like for something, a predilection

He also had a *penchant* for fussing with his toupee and clicking his dentures when he spoke.

PERMEATE v. to spread or seep through, to penetrate, to pervade

A strong hatred for Pierre Pinnacle began to *permeate* the principality of Swump.

PERUSE v. to study, to read over leisurely

When Pierre *perused* the *Swump Daily Times*, the editorials called for his downfall.

His *perusal* (n.) of the editorials revealed strong resentment towards his ideas.

PHILANTHROPY n. good will towards all people, love of mankind, act of generosity

Pierre Pinnacle was hurt that his charitable donations to hair growth clinics, acts of obvious *philanthropy*, were now being ignored.

His *philanthropic* (adj.) interests were clearly forgotten in the rush to overthrow him.

PIOUS adj. (PIE-US) reverent, devout, dutiful; may at times be marked by hypocrisy

Even the most *pious* citizens of Swump, those who had profited from Pierre's rule, felt they had to distance themselves from him.

PIQUE v. (PEEK) to hurt or rile the feelings of someone, irritate

Pierre Pinnacle was genuinely *piqued* by everyone's attitude, so he finally decided to unleash his super weapon for global destruction—the Nasal Bomb.

The world experienced some *pique* (n.) and three days of intense sinus draining because of Pierre Pinnacle's dastardly device.

Plug In

Plug in your answers to see if you've made the right word power connections. Finish the sentences below, using the following words from Lesson 14:

(a) osmosis	(f) pariah	(k) permeate
(b) ousted	(g) partition	(l) peruse
(c) overture	(h) paucity	(m) philanthropy
(d) palatable	(i) pedantic	(n) pious
(e) paltry	(j) penchant	(o) pique

1. Ryan decided to _____ the novel when he heard it hit the best-seller list.

2. Elliot had a _____ for cherry candies, which he ate every single day.

3. There was a _____ of food in the village, and many children went to bed hungry.

4. Mrs. Sexton found the food hardly _____ , but not wanting to insult her hostess she ate in anyway.

5. Angry, Skippy changed into a sweet little boy by _____ whenever he was around Uncle Sammy.

6. Dylan made an _____ to Dana, but she rejected him.

7. When Alan accused his boss of sexual harassment, he became a _____ , as no one wanted to believe him.

8. Todd was _____ from his position as secretary because he wrote down only what he believed and not what he heard.

9. The _____ in the middle of the room did not add to anyone's sense of privacy.

10. Professor Simpson was so _____ , no one could stand to listen.

11. A smell of unimaginable intensity began to _____ the room.

12. Joseph became quite _____ after attending St. Agnes' School.

13. Laura had a fit of _____ when told her job security was in question.

14. Ms. Tess Gallagher's _____ was celebrated at a dinner chaired by the head of her favorite charity.

15. The _____ amount of art supplies made it difficult for the children to express their creativity.

☀️ Recharge

Here are the answers to this quiz. Check to see if you made the right word power connections! Test yourself again on the ones you missed.

1.	l	6.	c	11.	k
2.	j	7.	f	12.	n
3.	h	8.	b	13.	o
4.	d	9.	g	14.	m
5.	a	10.	i	15.	e

A Provincial Precept
or a Pretentious Precept?

PIVOTAL adj. (PIV-UH-TUL) crucial, something around which things turn

Simon, who claimed to have wealthy contacts, promised to play a *pivotal* role in securing funds for the arts center, and so was given the title Executive Director.

PLACATE v. to soothe, to appease with concessions

Jeremy, an active and loyal member of the board, was seething with jealousy and had to be *placated* with the title, Senior Manager of Fund-Raising.

PLAUSIBLE adj. believable

It was not *plausible* that the two could work closely together; the rivalry between them was intense.

POIGNANT adj. (POIN-YANT) emotionally moving

Other than a *poignant* moment when Simon and Jeremy embraced at a co-worker's funeral, they simply could not get along.

It was a moment of great *poignancy* (n).

POLEMIC n. a powerful argument to defend a thesis

Simon had a tendency to deliver an endless *polemic* each time he presented a fund raising plan that others questioned.

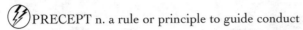

PRECEPT n. a rule or principle to guide conduct

Jeremy attempted to honor the *precept* that what mattered most was the arts center and not his own ego, but at times he wanted only to resign

PRECLUDE v. to make impossible, to shut out, to bar

Jeremy's sense of obligation *precluded* him from taking such drastic action.

PRETENTIOUS adj. (PRE-TEN-SHUS) showy, self-important, make unjustifiable claims to excellence

Simon unfortunately grew more and more *pretentious* each day, assuring everyone that with his superior fund-raising skills all would be well.

PROLIFIC adj. marked by abundant production or offspring

Jeremy decided to busy himself writing promotional materials and became quite *prolific* and skilled at this endeavor.

PROSAIC adj. (PRO-SAY-IK) dull, unimaginative, lacking excitement

Simon's written materials were paltry and *prosaic,* and inspired no one.

PROVINCIAL adj. (PRO-VIN-SHUL) limited in outlook, narrow in ideas

In fact, as time marched on, it struck everyone concerned that Simon's approach was rather *provincial,* in that it failed to take into account the interests of a broad audience.

PRUDENT adj. careful, cautious

Jeremy decided to behave in a *prudent* fashion, and keep his criticisms to himself.

He *prudently* (adv) decided to stay silent so as not to cause more problems.

QUAINT adj. pleasantly old-fashioned, picturesque

When asked what he thought of one of Simon's promotional materials, Jeremy, searching for something kind to say replied, "Well, it's *quaint.*"

QUELL v. to put an end to, to squelch, to calm

Finally, even Jeremy's measured words could not *quell* the dissatisfaction felt by the board, and so Simon was asked to relinquish his position.

QUINTESSENTIAL adj. the most perfect example of

Turning to Jeremy they apologetically proclaimed, "You are the *quintessential* fund-raiser, and we are sorry for not recognizing this fact early on."

Plug In

Plug in your answers to see if you've the right connections.
Match each word with its correct definition.

___ 1. PIVOTAL	(a) picturesque
___ 2. PLACATE	(b) to squelch
___ 3. PLAUSIBLE	(c) showy
___ 4. POIGNANT	(d) highly productive
___ 5. POLEMIC	(e) a powerful argument
___ 6. PRECEPT	(f) a perfect example
___ 7. PRECLUDE	(g) to soothe
___ 8. PRETENTIOUS	(h) emotionally touching
___ 9. PROLIFIC	(i) believable
___ 10. PROSAIC	(j) unoriginal
___ 11. PROVINCIAL	(k) central
___ 12. PRUDENT	(l) to make impossible
___ 13. QUAINT	(m) limited
___ 14. QUELL	(n) a standard by which to live
___ 15. QUINTESSENTIAL	(o) cautious

🔅 Recharge

Here are the answers to this quiz. Check to see if you made the right connections! Test yourself again on the ones you missed.

1.	k	6.	n	11.	m
2.	g	7.	l	12.	o
3.	i	8.	c	13.	a
4.	h	9.	d	14.	b
5.	e	10.	j	15.	f

Is Randi Raucous, Resilient, or Resplendent?

⚡ QUIXOTIC adj. (KWIX-OT-IC) foolishly impractical and idealistic

Randi had a *quixotic* nature and so was forever pursuing romantic dreams.

⚡ RAUCOUS adj. (RAW-CUSS) boisterous, harsh sounding, noisy and disorderly

Her younger brothers were a *raucous* bunch and often teased Randi unmercifully.

⚡ REBUFF v. to snub, to refuse in a blunt or rude way

As a result, when any of them needed her help, she would unceremoniously *rebuff* them, saying, "Are you kidding? The way you treat me?"

REBUKE v. to criticize or reprimand sharply

The parents often *rebuked* all the children for their lack of kindness towards each other.

RECIPROCAL adj. mutual, interchangeable, shared

"Kindness must be *reciprocal*," Randi would respond haughtily, "and I see no reason to help them when all I can expect is insults."

"If they would say one thing nice to me, I would *reciprocate* (v.) in kind," Randi assured her parents.

"I was nice the other day, and James was crude," Randi insisted "and so you can see there is no *reciprocity* (n.) between us."

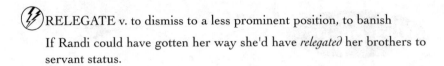
RELEGATE v. to dismiss to a less prominent position, to banish

If Randi could have gotten her way she'd have *relegated* her brothers to servant status.

RELIC n. an object associated with a saint, something that remains from the past

She considered her parent's ideas of equality *relics* from their flower-child pasts.

Her mother's program from a Jefferson Airplane concert was treated like a *relic* in that it was elaborately framed and hung in the foyer.

REPLENISH v. to refill, to supply once more

Occasionally Randi would run out of aspirations, and so to *replenish* her well of dreams she would peruse the newspaper looking for a new cause to take up or a new heroine to emulate.

REPREHENSIBLE adj. deserving of blame

Sometimes Randi would read of an atrocity that was so *reprehensible* she could barely sleep that night.

REPROVE v. to gently criticize

Her mother would *reprove* Randi at these times, and urge her to read light fiction instead.

RESCIND v. (RE-SIND) to cancel, to repeal

Randi would grow so indignant at the idea that she was incapable of handling hard news, that her mother would *rescind* the suggestion and simply say, "Fine. Read what interests you."

RESILIENT adj. an ability to recover from, or adjust easily

Randi's spirits were indeed *resilient*—after a sleepless night she would often sing and dance about the house.

Her *resilience* (n.) made it easy for Randi to cope with life's difficulties.

RESPITE n. (RES-PIT) an interval of rest, a temporary delay

Randi would occasionally take a *respite* from her reading and concentrate on goals such as winning a tennis tournament.

RESPLENDENT adj. brilliant, gloriously bright

Randi looked utterly *resplendent* holding the golden trophy above her head and smiling as if she might burst into song.

The photograph reflected a scene of great *resplendence* (n.).

ROBUST adj. strong and healthy, vigorous

Even Randi's brothers had to admit their sister had proven herself quite *robust,* capable of far more than fanciful dreams.

Plug In

Plug in your answers to see if you've the right connections.
Which sentences correctly use the above words?

1. Mr. Copley-Merta championed one quixotic cause after another, and predictably, the town began to flourish economically and socially.
   CORRECT   INCORRECT

2. The kindergarteners were so raucous that the teacher announced there would be no recess if they did not calm down.
   CORRECT   INCORRECT

3. Derek could not help but rebuff Jenny's advances for he had coveted her since the first time they met.
   CORRECT   INCORRECT

4. Sally rebuked her son for his intolerable behavior at the zoo.
   CORRECT   INCORRECT

5. Elaine's school had a reciprocal arrangement with Jenny's and so the girls often attended classes with each other.
   CORRECT   INCORRECT

6. Rosario was relegated to Chief Operating Officer after submitting an impressive plan for a major corporate reorganization.
   CORRECT   INCORRECT

7. Kevin pondered the ancient relic, trying to imagine the urn as it might have originally looked.
   CORRECT   INCORRECT

8. Andrea replenished the dish with candies so that all the children could have a piece.

        CORRECT   INCORRECT

9. Sam thought the criminal's actions were reprehensible, yet pitied him anyway.

        CORRECT   INCORRECT

10. Karl reproved her son for buying and selling drugs, and then promptly threw him out.

        CORRECT   INCORRECT

11. Once Anne Boleyn was beheaded, it was too late for Henry VIII to rescind the order.

        CORRECT   INCORRECT

12. Stephanie was deeply saddened by her puppy's demise, but her resilience was amazing and by the end of the month she was begging for a new pet.

        CORRECT   INCORRECT

13. Juanita decided it was time for a respite from her busy schedule and so she boarded a plane to Luxembourg.

        CORRECT   INCORRECT

14. Princess Kira was resplendent in a gown of chartreuse silk and Belgian lace.

        CORRECT   INCORRECT

15. Thomas had grown so robust that his friends could not do enough to cheer him up.

        CORRECT   INCORRECT

⚡ Recharge

Here are the answers to this quiz. Check to see if you made the right connections! Test yourself again on the ones you missed.

1. incorrect	6. incorrect	11. correct
2. correct	7. correct	12. correct
3. incorrect	8. correct	13. correct
4. correct	9. correct	14. correct
5. correct	10 incorrect	15. incorrect

Is Chris's Attitude Stoic or Sardonic?

RUSTIC adj. primitive, rural, lacking city comforts

Chris lived in a *rustic* cabin, miles from any shopping mall.

SACCHARINE adj. excessively sweet

His nearest neighbor, Sherry, was a *saccharine* young school teacher, who was continually slipping adoring and inappropriate messages under his door.

SARDONIC adj. disdainful, scornfully mocking

Chris made many *sardonic* remarks about her to his close friend Anthony, though he made no effort to put an end to her pursuit of him.

SCANTY adj. minimal, hardly sufficient

One evening Sherry knocked on his door wearing such a *scanty* pair of shorts that Chris was almost embarrassed to be in her presence.

SCINTILLATE v. to sparkle, to gleam, to be animated or brilliant

But as Sherry stood there, it occurred to Chris that her conversation, in person, was quite *scintillating*.

SERVILE adj. submissive, behaving like a slave

Before long a romance began and Chris became utterly *servile* in her presence, anxious to satisfy her every whim.

SLOTH n. sluggish, laziness, indolence

He stopped working, as he could concentrate on nothing but her, and after a time she became impatient with his *sloth*.

His *slothfulness* (adj.) began to drive her crazy.

SPURIOUS adj. false, fake, not genuine

Sherry began to devise *spurious* reasons for spending evenings without Chris, so that she could attend parties with other single people.

STAGNATE v. to lie inactive, to stay in one place

Chris began to sense their relationship was *stagnating,* so he attempted to rejuvenate it with a planned vacation to Mexico.

He did not realize the *stagnation* (n.) he was experiencing was of Sherry's design.

STATIC n. stationary, not changing or moving

"There is a *static* quality to our relationship because I'm not sure I want it to go any further," Sherry explained upon turning down the invitation. "Don't give me any *static*," she added.

STEADFAST adj. loyal, faithful

"Have I not been a *steadfast* companion? Have I not stood by you through thick and thin?" Chris asked, feeling horribly wounded.

STOIC adj. showing indifference to pain, apathetic

Chris finally decided to accept Sherry's decision and with a *stoic* attitude showed her to the door.

He then *stoically* (adv.) canceled the trip reservations without shedding a tear.

His *stoicism* was impressive, but it wasn't going to last.

STRATAGEM n. a trick or deceptive scheme

Days after Sherry left, Chris began to plan a *stratagem* to win her back, positive that she still loved him.

STRIDENT adj. loud, harsh, grating

Sherry however fell for none of his schemes, and soon Chris became *strident* in his insistence that she give their relationship another try.

STYMIE v. to get in the way of, to hinder, to block

But Chris was *stymied* by Sherry's immutability and when she finally admitted there was someone else, he was forced to return to his rustic cabin and have a good cry.

 Plug In

Plug in your answers to see if you've made the right connections. Choose the correct definition for each word.

1. RUSTIC
   a) refined
   b) primitive
   c) civilized

2. SACCHARINE
   a) intense
   b) submissive
   c) overly sweet

3. SARDONIC
   a) silly
   b) lazy
   c) scornful

4. SCANTY
   a) fake
   b) minimal
   c) inactive

5. SCINTILLATE
   a) to plan a trick
   b) to remain loyal
   c) to sparkle

6. SERVILE
   a) loyal
   b) noisy
   c) submissive

7. SLOTH
   a) laziness
   b) persistence
   c) indifference to pain

8. SPURIOUS
   a) bright
   b) fake
   c) stationary

9. STAGNATE
   a) to suffer pain
   b) to insist
   c) to stay inactive

10. STATIC
    a) energized
    b) stable
    c) unchanging

11. STEADFAST
    a) loyal
    b) unaffected by pain c) unmoved

12. STOIC
    a) insistent
    b) uncivilized
    c) suffers silently

13. STRATAGEM
   a) social strata
   b) a straightway
   c) a scheme

14. STRIDENT
   a) harsh
   b) lazy
   c) stuck

15. STYMIED
   a) frustrated
   b) curious
   c) cynical

⋅꣐⋅ *Recharge*

Here are the answers to this quiz. Check to see if you made the right connections! Test yourself again on the ones you missed.

1.	b	6.	c	11.	a
2.	c	7.	a	12.	c
3.	c	8.	b	13.	c
4.	b	9.	c	14.	a
5.	c	10.	c	15.	a

lesson 18

Politics—Tedious or Odious?

SUCCINCT adj. (SUK-SINKED) concise, clearly expressed with a few words

Governor Kunitz always tried to be *succinct* when participating in a campaign debate.

SURFEIT n. (SIR-FIT) abundance, excessive amount

His opponent, Tim O'Connor, always used a *surfeit* of hyperbole and figures.

SURMISE v. to infer on minimal grounds, conjecture, suppose

Governor Kunitz *surmised* that Tim was terribly insecure because otherwise he would have spoken with a simpler style.

TABLE v. to remove from consideration

At one point a debate between them grew so hostile and long winded that a moderator suggested they *table* the issue.

TEDIOUS adj. (TEE-DEE-US) boring, tiresome

Governor Kunitz in truth found making speeches, shaking hands, and constantly smiling terribly *tedious*.

The *tedium* (n.) of the campaign trail could be relentless.

TEEM v. to swarm, to be inundated, to become full to overflowing

His final campaign stop in one city was at an outdoor market which was *teeming* with schoolchildren from all over the area.

TEMPERANCE n. habitual moderation, the avoidance of excess

Governor Kunitz grew so annoyed that he craved a drink or two, but in the interest of *temperance,* he managed to squelch the desire.

⚡TENET n. a principle, doctrine or belief held as so by a group

He lived by the *tenet* that sound leadership required a sound mind.

⚡TENTATIVE adj. uncertain, temporary not fully worked out

Tim O'Connor, in contrast, was a very *tentative* personality, forever sounding as if he couldn't quite believe in his own political positions.

TENUOUS adj. flimsy, extremely thin, having little substance, lacking stability

Tim had only a *tenuous* understanding of what the people needed in a leader.

The *tenuousness* (n.) of his grasp did not bode well for his election.

TEPID adj. lukewarm, unenthusiastic, halfhearted

He began to realize how profoundly he had failed to win voter loyalty when he received a *tepid* welcome at his own headquarters upon his return from the campaign trail.

⚡TERSE adj. concise, brief, free of extra words

He made a few *terse* remarks and then retreated to a private room where he sat for a long time, head in hands.

THEOLOGY n. the study of God or religion

It occurred to Tim O'Connor that he should have majored in *theology* instead of political science in college, because had he done so he might now have understood better how to touch the hearts and minds of the public.

THWART v. to prevent from being accomplished, to frustrate, to hinder

> Of course Tim O'Connor's campaign had also been *thwarted* by his poor choice of staff.

TIRADE n. (TIE-RADE) a long and angry speech

> Finally, Tim re-entered the main hall, faced his loyal followers and delivered a *tirade* of such intensity, they all walked out, clearly relieved they had gotten him nowhere.

Plug In

Plug in your answers to see if you've made the right connections.

Match each word with its definition.

__ 1. SUCCINCT		(a)	lukewarm
__ 2. SURFEIT		(b)	a principle
__ 3. SURMISE		(c)	frustrate
__ 4. TABLE		(d)	swarm
__ 5. TEDIOUS		(e)	flimsy
__ 6. TEEM		(f)	infer
__ 7. TEMPERANCE		(g)	avoid excess
__ 8. TENET		(h)	concise
__ 9. TENTATIVE		(i)	excess
__ 10. TENUOUS		(j)	put aside
__ 11. TEPID		(k)	uncertain
__ 12. TERSE		(l)	brief
__ 13. THEOLOGY		(m)	study of religion
__ 14. THWART		(n)	boring
__ 15. TIRADE		(o)	angry speech

Recharge

Here are the answers to this quiz. Check to see if you made the right connections!

1.	h	6.	d	11.	a		
2.	i	7.	g	12.	l		
3.	f	8.	b	13.	m		
4.	j	9.	k	14.	c		
5.	n	10.	e	15.	o		

Was Tanya's Tryst a Tortuous Travesty or Just Trite?

TONIC n. a refreshing drink, something that invigorates

The countryside proved to be a *tonic* for Tanya's frazzled nerves.

TORTUOUS adj. (TOR-CHOO-WUS) winding, twisting, full of curves

The location of the inn was at the top of a *tortuous* road that wound in sharp curves up a steep mountain.

TOUT v. (TOWT) to brag publicly, to praise highly

The facility, with its hot springs and exercise room, had been *touted* as the perfect place for rest and relaxation.

TRANSFIX v. to cause to stand motionless with awe or other intense emotion

Tanya would regularly take walks in the sunshine, pausing at a certain rock where she would rest, *transfixed* by the profusion of wild flowers that swayed before her.

TRAVESTY n. a parody, an imitation that makes crude fun of something

She began to think that her old life, the one which had her working from seven in the morning to seven at night, was simply a *travesty*, for it was really no life at all.

TRITE adj. unoriginal, overused, cliched, commonplace

Tanya hated to be *trite* but when asked how she felt about going back home, she replied, "All work and no play makes Jill a dull girl."

TRIVIAL adj. unimportant, insignificant

She did not think it *trivial* that her headaches had all but disappeared at the inn.

Tanya did not wish to *trivialize* (v.) her old life, but still, there seemed little reason to go back.

TRYST n. (TRIST) a secret meeting of lovers

Of course it didn't hurt that Tanya was enjoying a regular *tryst* with the town's most eligible bachelor, Tommy Lee.

TUMULT n. noisy commotion, uproar

Tanya was happy to hide away at the inn, with her occasional lover, and keep the *tumult* of her old life far away with all its familial and work responsibilities.

TURPITUDE adj. shameful wickedness, evil, depravity

The local gossip mongers discovered Tommy Lee and Tanya were having an affair; being provincial in outlook, they deemed the affair an act of unforgivable *turpitude*.

UNDERMINE v. to weaken the support of, to injure in a slow or sneaky way

The rumors began to *undermine* their relationship and pretty soon Tommy Lee, who lived in town all year round and who was actually rather spineless, decided to end the affair.

UNILATERAL adj. on one side alone

It was a *unilateral* decision, and Tanya was infuriated at the way in which Tommy Lee came to this decision on his own.

URBANE adj. suave, sophisticated, polished

Tanya began to miss the more *urbane* men back in the city—men who would not be swayed in any way by the opinions of others.

USURP v. to seize wrongfully

She felt Tommy Lee had *usurped* her right to stand firm against the opinions of others.

⚡ VAPID adj. (VAP-ID) tasteless, dull

Ultimately, Tanya decided life on top of a mountain could be pretty *vapid*, and so she packed her bags to return home, sad, but determined to improve her old life.

🚦 Plug In

Plug in your answers to see if you've made the right connections.
Fill in the blanks.

1. The plot was so _____ that Julia could not follow the action at all.

2. It was a _____ thing to be sure, but Jon could not help being annoyed when his girlfriend laughed like a hyena.

3. Marshall considered it a _____ that James with his poor grades and lack of motivation got into Harvard, but Logan, the more ambitious of the two, did not.

4. There was too much _____ in the playroom for Mr. Mura to work on the computer, so he left the kids to their pillow fight and went upstairs.

5. Rachel felt _____ by her mother's insistence on telling her what to wear each morning.

6. Nathan's dad made a _____ decision to sign him up for baseball, choosing not to listen his protests.

7. It was _____ to Shalena's ears when Juan professed his undying love.

8. Charles was _____ by the headhunter as the most productive CEO of the year.

9. Wendy and Tony had a _____ at the most elegant hotel in Boston.

10. His crime was such an act of _____ that Ben's own mother could not look him in the eye.

11. Archie was _____ by Camille's smile.

12. Shawna had a way with words, but her sister Anna Louisa could be, in contrast, unbelievably _____.

13. Eddy came off as _____, but was really just a mama's boy.

14. Loretta concerned herself primarily with her looks, and so she came off as incredibly _____.

15. The king's power was _____ by his cousin the Duchess of Vendler who had always been hungry for the crown.

💡 Recharge

Here are the answers to this quiz. Check to see if you made the right connections! Test yourself again on the ones you missed.

1. tortuous	6. unilateral	11. transfixed
2. trivial	7. tonic	12. trite
3. travesty	8. touted	13. urbane
4. tumult	9. tryst	14. vapid
5. undermined	10. turpitude	15. usurped

Is Van Virulently Verbose?

VEHEMENT adj. intense, forceful, marked by strong feeling

Anna was *vehement* about her dislike for her cousin Van.

She was *vehemently* (adv.) opposed to his illegal activities.

VERBOSE adj. wordy

She also found him to be unbearably *verbose* and would often simply turn away when he began speaking.

His *verbosity* (n.) drove her crazy.

VESTIGE n. the remains of something that no longer exists

Anna's anger, she had to admit, was a *vestige* of the days when they were little kids and Van used to tease her mercilessly about her looks, calling her Orphan Annie.

VIABLE adj. workable, capable of living and growing, able to succeed

She also knew that Van was a rather stupid fellow and had worked out no *viable* way to make a living.

VIE v. to compete, to contest

He did however have a way with the ladies, many of whom were always *vying* for his attention.

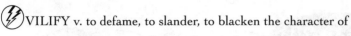

VILIFY v. to defame, to slander, to blacken the character of

Anna found his popularity so absurd, that she would on occasion *vilify* him to one of his lovers.

Vilifying him, in fact, gave her great pleasure and relief.

VIRULENT adj. extremely poisonous, malignant, full of hate

Van would of course become *virulent* with rage when Anna's words got back to him and he would hurl such painful insults upon her that she could barely stand it.

VIVACIOUS adj. lively, spirited

The truth is Anna was tremendously *vivacious* and fun to be with, but her looks were a real problem.

VOLATILE adj. explosive, tends to burn quickly

Anna had a long nose and curly red hair, and she would become quite *volatile* if anyone commented upon these features.

She was known for her *volatility* if anyone criticized her looks.

WANTON adj. immoral, lewd, deliberate maliciousness, having no regard for others

Van launched *wantonly* (adv.) into a tirade about Anna's hair that left her weeping uncontrollably.

WAVER v. to be indecisive or inconstant, to fluctuate in opinion

He did not *waver* for a moment and, upon seeing her tears, burst into further expletives, this time ridiculing her nose.

WINSOME adj. charming, sweetly engaging

Jillian, the most *winsome* of Van's girlfriends, overheard his tirade and urgently begged him to stop.

WISTFUL adj. yearning, sad longing, a gentle desire

Jillian grew *wistful* for her old boyfriend Alan as a direct result of Van's obscene behavior.

ZEALOT n. a person with great enthusiasm for and commitment to a cause

But Alan had become a *zealot,* championing the cause of the environment, and had moved out West.

He was so *zealous* (adj.) in his beliefs that he could countenance no one who failed to understand the plight of the earth.

ZENITH n. the highest point

Van was arrested by an officer who, upon meeting Anna at the courthouse, fell in love with her. His marriage proposal was the *zenith* of Anna's life.

Plug In

Plug in your answers to see if you've made the right connections. Let's try this again. Match the word closest to the word that means the opposite.

__	1. VEHEMENT	(a)	kindly
__	2. VERBOSE	(b)	unworkable
__	3. VESTIGE	(c)	compliment
__	4. VIABLE	(d)	unsentimental
__	5. VIE	(e)	disinterested party
__	6. VILIFY	(f)	constant
__	7. VIRULENT	(g)	weak
__	8. VIVACIOUS	(h)	the lowest point
__	9. VOLATILE	(i)	give up
__	10. WANTON	(j)	kind attention
__	11 WAVER	(k)	present abundance
__	12. WINSOME	(l)	loathsome
__	13. WISTFUL	(m)	serene
__	14. ZEALOT	(n)	terse
__	15. ZENITH	(o)	lethargic

⌖Recharge

Here are the answers to this quiz. Check to see if you made the right connections! Test yourself again on the ones you missed.

1.	g	6.	c	11.	f
2.	n	7.	a	12.	l
3.	k	8.	o	13.	d
4.	b	9.	m	14.	e
5.	i	10.	j	15.	h

SECTION 2

Words to the Second Power: Harder Words You Really Ought to Know

With Accolades or Accouterments?

ABEYANCE n. (A-BAY-ANSE) a temporary suspension of activity

Michelle held her excitement in *abeyance* while the college review board considered her application.

ABROGATE v. to repeal, to set aside, to nullify

They had agreed to *abrogate* their initial decision, when it was discovered that a piece of her original application had been misplaced.

ABSCOND v. to leave quickly and secretively

Some mischievous, and subsequently expelled, student had *absconded* one night with a pile of applications simply to make trouble.

ABSTINENCE n. voluntarily refraining from eating certain foods or drink, or from doing something pleasant but not good for you.

Michelle was tempted to find the student who had done this and kick him where it hurts, but she decided *abstinence* was the wiser route.

Michelle *abstained* (v.) from calling the student and verbally abusing him.

ABSTRUSE adj. (AB-STROOSE) hard to understand or grasp

The student attempted to explain himself but his reasons were so *abstruse* that everyone in a position of authority tuned out.

ACCOLADE n. award or honor, high praise

Shortly thereafter Michelle received a call from the admissions office;

they heaped *accolades* upon her application essay.

ACCOUTERMENTS n. (A-KOOTER-MONTS) personal clothing, acces-sories, or equipment

Michelle promptly prepared to pack up all the necessary *accouterments* she would need for a year at the most prestigious college in the country.

ACQUIT v. (A-KWIT) to find not guilty, to conduct oneself

She wished to be well equipped for a campus lifestyle, as well as to *acquit* herself in a worldly and sophisticated fashion.

The student was not *acquitted* of the crime and found himself both expelled and heavily fined.

ADJURE v. to command or urge solemnly and earnestly

Michelle's father *adjured* her to make him proud as she was the first woman in the family to make it into such an illustrious institution.

ⓩADUMBRATE v. to suggest partly, to give a hint of things to come, to fore-shadow vaguely

It was clear Michelle's father was attempting to moderate his expecta-tions of her so as not to intimidate her, and so he *adumbrated* for most of the hour.

AEGIS n. (A-JISS) protection, patronage

"You will no longer be under my *aegis*," he began carefully," and so I hope you will conduct yourself in a safe and intelligent manner."

AGGRIEVE v. to distress, to mistreat

"Please do not *aggrieve* me in any way," he continued, "as I have worked many years to see this day."

AKIMBO adj. having one's hands in a bent position on the hips, or figuratively speaking, something slightly out of balance

Michelle stood quietly, arms *akimbo*, listening unhappily to her father's words.

She noticed his hat was slightly *akimbo*, but she chose to say nothing.

ALACRITY adj. cheerful readiness, liveliness or eagerness

Michelle was so happy when her father was through with his little speech that she decided to take a walk, skipping out the door with great *alacrity.*

ALCHEMY n. (AL-KE-MEE) a process of transformation that is seemingly magical

Half way down the block it occurred to Michelle that it might take a touch of *alchemy* to give her the confidence and sophistication she would need to meet her dad's expectations . . . and so she headed for the beauty salon.

Plug In

Plug in your answers to see if you've made the right connections.
Match the word with its correct definition.

__ 1. ABEYANCE	(a)	distress
__ 2. ABROGATE	(b)	to entreat urgently
__ 3. ABSCOND	(c)	a temporary suspension
__ 4. ABSTINENCE	(d)	magical transformation
__ 5. ABSTRUSE	(e)	hands on hips
__ 6. ACCOLADE	(f)	high praise
__ 7. ACCOUTERMENTS	(g)	to nullify
__ 8. ACQUIT	(h)	to find not guilty
__ 9. ADJURE	(i)	to leave secretively
__ 10. ADUMBRATE	(j)	sponsorship
__ 11. AEGIS	(k)	voluntarily refraining from
__ 12. AGGRIEVE	(l)	personal accessories
__ 13. AKIMBO	(m)	happiness
__ 14. ALACRITY	(n)	to vaguely indicate
__ 15. ALCHEMY	(o)	unclear

⚙·Recharge

Here are the answers to this quiz. Check to see if you made the right connections! Test yourself again on the ones you missed.

1) c   6) f   11) j
2) g   7) l   12) a
3) i   8) h   13) e
4) k   9) b   14) m
5) o   10) n   15) d

Is this Therapist Assiduous, Ascetic, or Apoplectic?

AMBULATORY adj. (AM-BYOU-LA-TORY) able to walk or move about

After the accident LaDonna was not *ambulatory*, and spent many hours restlessly in bed.

She could not *ambulate* (v.).

AMELIORATE v. (A-MEEL-EE-OR-ATE) to make better, to ease or improve

Her boredom was *ameliorated* by the fabulously handsome doctor who would occasionally stop by to check her vital signs.

ANATHEMA n. (AN-ATH-UH-MAH) something or someone loathed or intensely disliked

Lying still was an *anathema* to LaDonna because she led a very physically active life.

ANCILLARY adj. (ANS-ILL-ARY) subsidiary, subordinate

She received physical therapy as an *ancillary* service to help get her back on her feet.

ANOMIE n. (AN-O-MEE) instability caused by an erosion of values or lack of purpose

LaDonna couldn't wait to leave the hospital as she sensed a certain *anomie* in the hall due to recent personnel cuts. Patients cared for under condition of such *anomie* often do not get the attention they need.

ANTIPODAL adj. (AN-TIP-UH-DULL) situated on opposite sides of the earth, or being exactly opposite

LaDonna's hospital roommate took an *antipodal* position on what seemed to be happening as she felt more than satisfied with her care.

APOCRYPHAL adj. (A-POCK-RE-FULL) false, spurious, of doubtful origin

LaDonna began hearing stories of such medical mismanagement from other patients that she wondered if they were not *apocryphal* and simply born of fear.

APOGEE n. the point at which an orbiting object is farthest from what is being orbited, or the apex of something

Just as LaDonna reached the *apogee* of her frustration, she suddenly began to move with a bit more ease.

APOPLEXY n. a stroke resulting from loss of blood to the brain, becoming so angry as to be on the verge of exploding

LaDonna almost gave her physical therapist *apoplexy* when she was using the potentially dangerous therapeutic equipment all by herself.

She became *apoplectic* (adj.) and sharply cried out, "STOP. NOW!"

APOSTASY n. abandonment of a loyalty or religion

LaDonna was hurt by what she experienced as the *apostasy* of her therapist, who, in her mind, should have been thrilled about LaDonna's independence.

ARBITER n. a judge, one who decides

"I believe I am in a better position to be the *arbiter* of your progress than you," the therapist snapped, with a mixture of anger and anxiety.

ASCETIC adj. (AS-SET-TIC) hermitlike, self-denial, austere

"You want me to live an *ascetic* life," LaDonna cried out slightly irrationally, "shut up in my little hospital room with no pleasures of any kind!"

ASSIDUOUS adj. hardworking, busy, diligent

"No," the therapist explained, "but I am *assiduous* about what I do and that must include monitoring your use and progress on this equipment."

ASSIGNATION n. a secret meeting, a tryst, or something assigned

"If you must know," LaDonna finally admitted, "I have an *assignation* on the roof this evening with the most adorable doctor—we are going to share a bottle of champagne, and I did so want to walk towards him!"

"Well, you may transfer my responsibility for you to him by simple *assignation*," the therapist said, sarcastically handing over an official form.

BACCHANAL n. (BAC-AN-NAHL) a drunken reveler or orgy

"Of course," she added, with a twinkle in her eye, "It might have been polite to invite me to your little *bacchanal*!"

Plug In

Plug in your answers to see if you've made the right connections. Which sentences are correct?

1. Kate was now completely ambulatory and so had to be carried everywhere.
   CORRECT   INCORRECT

2. Sue wanted to ameliorate her son's pain, but there was nothing she could do as the infection had to take its course.
   CORRECT   INCORRECT

3. Chocolate was such an anathema to Don that he stuck a piece in his mouth at every opportunity.
   CORRECT   INCORRECT

4. The English Department was ancillary to the liberal arts program.
   CORRECT   INCORRECT

5. The sense of anomie in the streets was so intense, Marvin decided to grab the first cab he saw and speed homeward.
   CORRECT   INCORRECT

6. Gabrielle's color sense was completely antipodal to those of her sister, as she loved pastels, and her sister stuck to black and white.

         CORRECT   INCORRECT

7. "Such an apocryphal story!" Vic exclaimed as he listened to his younger brother describe his recent abduction by aliens.

         CORRECT   INCORRECT

8. Glenda reached the apogee of joy as she mounted the podium to accept her reward.

         CORRECT   INCORRECT

9. "You're going to give me apoplexy!" Julie smiled, as her sister continued describing the museum trip.

         CORRECT   INCORRECT

10. T.J. was secretly crushed by the apostasy of his right-hand man.

         CORRECT   INCORRECT

11. "I am the arbiter of good taste," Lynn proclaimed as she aggressively thrust her own vision for interior design on her hapless cousin.

         CORRECT   INCORRECT

12. Betty described herself as an ascetic, as she led her friends on a tour of her luxurious home.

         CORRECT   INCORRECT

13. Charles studied assiduously for the test and so his excellent grade was well deserved.

         CORRECT   INCORRECT

14. The two companies were scheduled for a highly publicized assignation later in the week.

         CORRECT   INCORRECT

15. Cynthia could not wait for the bacchanal she was planning the moment her parents left for France.

         CORRECT   INCORRECT

The answer key appears on the following page.

⌾ *Recharge*

Here are the answers to this quiz. Check to see if you made the right connections! Test yourself again on the ones you missed.

1. incorrect
2. correct
3. incorrect
4. incorrect
5. correct

6. correct
7. correct
8. correct
9. incorrect
10. correct

11. correct
12. incorrect
13. correct
14. incorrect
15. correct

Was the Bathos Bilious?

BANDY v. to toss back and forth, to exchange, to use in a glib way

The director and the producer *bandied* about the idea of using a complete unknown for the lead, while many an illustrious actor waited for them to settle down and make up their minds.

BATHOS n. a transition from the illustrious to the commonplace, overdone pathos, triteness

One particular actor was quite impressive during her audition but then dived into *bathos* when she began the teary, "I'll do anything for this part" routine.

BEHEMOTH n. (BE-HEE-MUTH) something that is enormous, or monstrous in size and power

The budget for the film had become a *behemoth*, staggering even the director, who was not sure the movie would ultimately earn out.

BELIE v. to run counter to, to show something as false

The director's confident demeanor, however, *belied* any rumors that he thought the film might be the biggest flop the studio had ever backed.

BESMIRCH v. to stain or soil (commonly as to reputation)

No one wished to *besmirch* the reputation of the two supporting actors, though they were generally thought to be examples of unwise casting.

BILIOUS adj. (BIL-YUS) ill-tempered, cranky, angry

The *bilious* remarks of the anxious studio head were so offensive to the producer that he respectfully requested not to be directly addressed by him again.

The *biliousness* (n.) of Max Walker, in fact, was so ugly that his own partner and brother left the offices for a round of golf.

BIVOUAC n. (BIV-O-ACK) a temporary encampment

Meanwhile about a dozen actors *bivouacked* right outside the studio gates, in an effort to secure auditions for the coveted role.

BON VIVANT n. (BON-VEE-VON) someone who enjoys luxurious living

The casting director had a reputation for being a major *bon vivant*.

BOWDLERIZE v. (BOW-DLER-EYES) to censor prudishly

The film was to be rated G, so the film editors and script writers were charged with the loathsome job of *bowdlerizing* the original witty but dicey dialogue.

BROOK v. to tolerate, to put up with something

Max Walker would *brook* no argument when it came to making the film appropriate for both children and adults.

BUMPTIOUS adj. (BUMP-SHUS) pushy, conceited, noisily self-assertive

The novelist, upon whose book the film was based, took a *bumptious* approach to the script discussions, arrogantly insisting that it echo his book page for page.

BYZANTINE adj. (BIZ-AN-TEEN) extremely intricate or complicated in structure

"Your novel," the director insisted, "is a fine work, but the plot is so *byzantine* that to try and recreate that in a film would result in a confusing jumble of unusable footage."

CABAL n. a secret group of conspirators, a clique

The production crew formed a *cabal* to undermine the author whose contract, mostly because he was Max Walker's nephew, unfortunately allowed him script "consultation."

CACHET n. (CASH-AY) a mark of distinction, a quality that "says" prestige

Standing up to Max Walker conferred a certain *cachet* on a person, though it did not do much for job security.

CALUMNY n. (KAL-UM-NEE) slander, deliberate false statements

When the director understood the degree of *calumny* his film was attracting, he called a news conference and informed the press that his film would be the year's most successful . . . and then he went back to his office and fired every one in sight.

Plug In

Plug in your answers to see if you've made the right connections.
Choose the correct definition for each word.

1. BANDY
   a) tolerate
   b) soil
   c) toss back and forth

2. BATHOS
   a) a downward spiral
   b) stupidity
   c) overdone pathos

3. BEHEMOTH
   a) legendary
   b) tremendously complex
   c) huge

4. CALUMNY
   a) conspirators
   b) bad luck
   c) slander

5. BYZANTINE
   a) very cruel
   b) tremendously complex
   c) morally offensive

6. BELIE
   a) hides

b) runs counter to
c) illustrates

7. BESMIRCH
   a) to stain
   b) to tease
   c) to tolerate

8. CABAL
   a) a club
   b) a group of conspirators
   c) a political party

9. CACHET
   a) a tent
   b) a hiding place
   c) a prestigious quality

10. BOWDLERIZE
    a) to make bawdy
    b) to censor
    c) to edit

11. BILIOUS
    a) pushy
    b) luxurious
    c) ill-tempered

12. BIVOUAC
    a) temporary shelter
    b) fortress
    c) luxury

13. BON VIVANT
    a) a slanderer
    b) a good appetite
    c) a high-life lover

14. BROOK
    a) to cross
    b) to sail
    c) to tolerate

15. BUMPTIOUS
    a) loudly assertive
    b) uneven
    c) incredibly annoying

☀ Recharge

Here are the answers to this quiz. Check to see if you made the right connections!

1)	c	6)	b	11)	c
2)	c	7)	a	12)	a
3)	c	8)	b	13)	c
4)	c	9)	c	14)	c
5)	b	10)	b	15)	a

Was the Conflagration Chemical or Chimerical?

CAPRICIOUS adj. (KA-PRI-SHUS) whimsical, fanciful, impulsive

Martina was often thought of as *capricious* since she frequently changed her mind about everything for no particular reason.

CASTIGATE v. to punish, chastise, criticize severely

Her boyfriend would often *castigate* Martina for her whimsical decisions, such as the time she booked tickets to Paris, and then suddenly decided she'd rather hike in the Rocky Mountains.

CATACLYSM n. (CAT-A-CLI-ZIM) a violent upheaval, an earthquake, a flood

Martina did have one enduring fantasy that included being air-lifted to a *cataclysm* so that she could experience "nature's fierceness."

She fancied the event as the zenith of excitement, and failed to appreciate the *cataclysmic* (adj.) effects the violence could have on peoples' lives.

CAVIL v. (KAV-UL) to quibble, to raise trivial objections

Once, after a catastrophic flash flood, Martina tried to rent a helicopter, but when the pilot protested, she snootily snapped, "Oh, stop *cavilling*."

CHARY adj. (CHAR-EE) careful, cautious, wary

The pilot was *chary* of expeditions into dangerous areas as he had seen too many horrific accidents.

⚡CHICANERY n. (SHI-CANE-ERY) deception or trickery

Martina toyed with the idea of using *chicanery* to get the pilot to fly, but at the last moment her capriciousness won out and she decided a trip to Rio would be more fun.

⚡CHIMERICAL adj. (KI-MER-I-CAL) wildly fanciful, absurd

She understood this sudden switch in plans might be seen as *chimerical*, and so she decided to try and make it sound profoundly logical.

⚡CIRCUMLOCUTION n. wordy language, an indirect, roundabout expression

Martina spoke with such *circumlocution* in an effort to confuse the pilot into agreeing to the flight, that he simply turned and walked away.

CLOUT n. (CLOWT) influence, a forceful blow

Martina resisted the urge to give him a *clout* on the head.

This was wise, as the pilot had a lot of *clout* with the airport personnel and she desperately needed someone to fly her to Rio.

COGITATE v. to ponder over, to mediate, to think

Martina sat down at the airport bar and after *cogitating* about her destination typically decided that perhaps Aspen was a better vacation spot.

COMPORT v. to behave

A ski vacation seemed perfect and the only question now was how to *comport* herself in a way that secured herself a quick trip.

COMPUNCTION n. remorse, feeling uneasy after having done something

Martina experienced no *compunction* over the way she treated the pilot as she found his conservative nature extremely annoying.

CONCOMITANT adj. accompanying, attending, going along with

Of course there was the *concomitant* problem of how to convince her boyfriend that Aspen was the place to be.

CONFLAGRATION n. a large, disastrous fire

Martina stared through the airport window thoughtfully, and suddenly

spotted a *conflagration* near the runway that was apparently so sudden, people were running everywhere in a panic.

CONTENTIOUS adj. argumentative over a point, quarrelsome

Everyone around her became extremely *contentious* over the question of how the fire started, but Martina was disinterested in all that.

It was her *contention* (n.) that the fire was a cataclysmic event and that, since she was there, was enough for her.

Plug In

Plug in your answers to see if you've made the right connections.
Which of these sentences are correct?

1. Ms. Yang made many a capricious decision, making it difficult for anyone to trust her inclinations.

CORRECT   INCORRECT

2. Mary Louisa castigated her brother for winning the tournament and making his family so proud.

CORRECT   INCORRECT

3. The rainstorm was a cataclysm, as it shut down schools for half a day and flooded several roads.

CORRECT   INCORRECT

4. The lawyers cavilled in front of the impatient judge who finally insisted that the court be adjourned.

CORRECT   INCORRECT

5. Chai was very chary when it came to new dates, as he was never sure he'd be comfortable.

CORRECT   INCORRECT

6. Chicanery was the only way Melissa felt she could win the attentions of Nate, the gorgeous new boy in school.

CORRECT   INCORRECT

7. But Melissa's chimerical budgeting plans were grounded firmly in reality.

CORRECT   INCORRECT

8.   The student spoke with such circumlocution that the professor could not understand what she was being asked . . . if anything.
     CORRECT   INCORRECT

9.   Dexter had so much clout with the head of the transportation union that the two of them could hardly be in the same room together.
     CORRECT   INCORRECT

10. The accountant needed to cogitate over the best way to preserve his client's financial windfall.
     CORRECT   INCORRECT

11. The little girl comported herself in such a sophisticated manner that it was easy to forget her young age.
     CORRECT   INCORRECT

12. The pianist not only won first place for his performance, but earned a concomitant prize for most affable contestant.
     CORRECT   INCORRECT

13. Lori experienced almost no compunction during her party as she was running a very high fever.
     CORRECT   INCORRECT

14. The conflagration seemed to light up the night's sky.
     CORRECT   INCORRECT

15. The discussion was so contentious that both parties couldn't help laughing and joking as they moved through the meeting's agenda.
     CORRECT   INCORRECT

 **Recharge**

Here are the answers to this quiz. Check to see if you made the right connections!

1) correct	6) correct	11) correct
2) incorrect	7) incorrect	12) correct
3) incorrect	8) correct	13) incorrect
4) correct	9) incorrect	14) correct
5) correct	10) correct	15) incorrect

Is a Diaspora a Deleterious Debacle?

CORTEGE n. (CORE-TEJ) a procession, a group of attendants

Queen Kristin walked the winding street of her principality, a *cortege* of ladies-in-waiting behind her.

COTERIE n. (CO-TUR-EE) an intimate group of people with a common interest

Her *coterie* of friends stayed behind, as this was an official occasion.

COVET v. (CUV-ET) to wish for with envy

One friend in particular could not bear to watch the pomp and circumstance because she so fiercely *coveted* the crown herself.

She was *covetous* (adj.) of the crown.

⚡DEBACLE n. (DEB-A-CUL) a disaster or violent breakdown

This friend, Siri, knew that if she attempted to dethrone Queen Kristin, it would be a *debacle* for the principality.

DECIMATE v. (DES-I-MATE) to kill or destroy a large part of

A revolution would *decimate* the population leaving the land barren and ruined.

Siri did not want the *decimation* (n.) blamed on her.

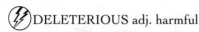

DELETERIOUS adj. harmful

And of course, if she lost her quest for the crown, the attempt to over-throw Kristin would be quite *deleterious* to her reputation as a loyal friend to say the least.

DEPREDATE v. to prey upon, to plunder with violence if necessary

Siri did, however, *depredate* Queen Kristin, by secretively stealing money from the treasury for all manner of personal luxury.

She considered it an act of only mild *depredation,* as there were many times she could have waltzed off with the crown jewels but chose not to.

DESCRY v. to discern, to see something , to catch sight of

The truth is Queen Kristin *descried* her friend's disloyalty years ago but felt it wiser to keep her close than to forge an outright rivalry between them.

DESICCATE: v. to dry out

Besides, a drought that had descended upon the land was now *desiccat-ing* the crops—Queen Kristin had more important problems to resolve.

The *desiccation* (n.) of the crops threatened the very existence of the principality.

DETERMINISM n. a philosophy that says things are determined in ways that are out of human hands

An attempt to save the crops proved to be a losing battle and so Queen Kristin, adopting a mode of *determinism,* simply hoped that luck would change.

DIASPORA n. the breaking up of the Jewish community in the sixth century where they were exiled from Israel, any dispersion of a people with a common origin

She also worried about an imminent *diaspora* of her people in far away regions as a result of famine at home.

DICHOTOMY n. (DI-COT-OMEE) division into two often contradictory parts

Siri saw her situation as a *dichotomy.*

DILETTANTE n. (DIL-E-TONT) a dabbler, someone with a superficial knowledge (usually of the arts)

Siri ultimately decided to remain a *dilettante* and not a political activist; instead of stealing the crown, she studied water color painting, occasionally.

DISCOMFIT v. to confuse, deceive

Queen Kristin was so *discomfited* by the news that her subjects were planning to desert the principality that she too withdrew from public life and arranged for elections.

DISQUIET v. to make uneasy

Ironically, doing so had a disquieting effect on her people who pushed up their plans for departure.

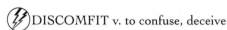Plug In

Plug in your answers to see if you've made the right connections. Match each word with the words or phrases that best describe its opposite. (Clearly there are no exact opposites, but that makes this more interesting . . . not to mention more thought provoking . . . something you may or may not welcome.)

__ 1. CORTEGE	(a) to not notice
__ 2. COTERIE	(b) to build
__ 3. COVET	(c) to be disinterested in
__ 4. DEBACLE	(d) to build confidence
__ 5. DECIMATE	(e) constructive
__ 6. DELETERIOUS	(f) irrigate
__ 7. DEPREDATE	(g) a sticking to the homeland
__ 8. DESCRY	(h) protect
__ 9. DESICCATE	(i) philosophy of personal responsibility
__ 10. DETERMINISM	(j) oneness
__ 11. DIASPORA	(k) a serious artiste
__ 12. DICHOTOMY	(l) an extremely positive event
__ 13. DILETTANTE	(m) put at ease
__ 14. DISCOMFIT	(n) a single follower
__ 15. DISQUIET	(o) a gathering of those who disagree

☀Recharge

Here are the answers to this quiz. Check to see if you made the right connections!

1)	n	6)	e	11)	g
2)	o	7)	h	12)	j
3)	c	8)	a	13)	k
4)	l	9)	f	14)	d
5)	b	10)	i	15)	m

lesson 26

Is Diurnal Ennui Endemic in Transylvania?

DISSIPATE v. to break up, to squander, to indulge excessively in sensual pleasure

The vampire *dissipated* his night hours drinking the blood of hapless villagers.

Count Igor lead a life of complete *dissipation* (n.).

DIURNAL adj. (DIE-EARN-UL) occurring during the day, happens every day

The *diurnal* habits of the next door neighbors were of little consequence to the Count, as he was snug in his coffin the moment the sun began to rise.

DOFF v. to take off (usually clothing) as a sign of greeting

Once, at midnight, Count Igor saw his neighbor, Mr. Torres, *doff* his hat at a passing young lady who merely smiled delicately at the gesture.

DOGGEREL n. comic, sometimes crude, informal verse

Count Igor thought the lady, Ms. Madeleine, so beauteous that he sent her a note which he later heard her describe as utter *doggerel.*

DOSSIER n. a file of documents, letters and records

The Count, undeterred, was so smitten that he decided to begin a *dossier* on the lady which would help him keep track of her every nocturnal move.

DRACONIAN adj. severe, exceedingly harsh

He knew if his designs on her were to be unearthed, he would be subjected to *draconian* measures that made even him shudder with fear.

⚡DULCET adj. (DUL-SET) having a nice, agreeable, melodious sound

His speaking voice was *dulcet* in tone and so he taped a romantic message for her to enjoy on her cassette player.

EFFETE adj. (EF-FEET) exhausted, lost vitality, overrefined

Madeleine found Igor in daylight a rather *effete* intellectual.

ELAN n. (AY-LON) vigor, distinctive, elegant style

Count Igor moved about at night with wonderful *elan,* and one evening Madeleine noticed him doing so with particular exuberance.

He had such *elan* that Madeleine could not help admiring his look and wondering where he had spent his formative years.

ELLIPTICAL adj. oval, obscure in expression

She noticed he traced an *elliptical* path around his castle, pausing only to admire the occasional bat that flew overhead.

Madeleine approached the count but spoke in such a nervous and *elliptical* fashion that even she could not determine what it was she was trying to say.

⚡ENCOMIUM n. a eulogy or expression of high praise

She murmured her apologies but he lavished such *encomium* upon her, that Madeleine immediately understood he desired her above all others.

⚡ENDEMIC adj. native, belonging to a specific region

Count Igor pointed to a particularly large bat hovering nearby, commenting it was *endemic* to the area.

ENERVATE v. to weaken, to sap the strength

As the night wore on and their conversation deepened Madeleine noticed the Count appeared *enervated* by their encounter, and wondered if she was talking too much.

ENNUI n. (ON-WEE) boredom, listlessness, lack of interest

The last thing she wished to inspire in her amorous new suitor was *ennui*.

ENSCONCE v. to settle in snugly, to hide in a secure place

Moments later Count Igor invited Madeleine back to his home for a nightcap, and sadly, shortly thereafter, the two of them were *ensconced* in his coffin.

Plug In

Plug in your answers to see if you've made the right connections.
Fill in the correct word for each sentence below.

(a) elan	(f) ensconced	(k) endemic
(b) dossier	(g) ennui	(l) elliptical
(c) diurnal	(h) dissipate	(m) encomium
(d) doffed	(i) enervated	(n) draconian
(e) doggerel	(j) effete	(o) dulcet

1. Mark drank so much, he began to _____ his chances for success.

2. Janet's puppy, a _____ animal woke up every morning at six.

3. Mr. Antonioni _____ his cap in a friendly manner as he passed the mail-man.

4. Mickey's speech was riddled with such _____ he was asked to leave the podium.

5. Once the newly married couple were happily _____ in their new home, they began to throw dinner parties.

6. Amy thought she would die of _____ if something exciting didn't happen.

7. Dina was so _____ by the race, she could hardly stand.

8. Those flowers are _____ to the swamp.

9. Her reasoning was so _____ no one could follow it.

10. The president offered his staff an endless _____ for their loyalty and diligence in the face of all odds.

11. The captive felt his treatment had been _____ and once released demanded recompense.

12. Shug dressed with such _____ everyone tried to emulate her.

13. When Meg unlocked his desk she found a _____ on herself an inch thick which included photographs and all manner of document.

14. Genevieve sang such a _____ song, it made the audience weep.

15. "You are an _____ pain in the neck," screeched the bag lady at the salesperson.

⚙·Recharge

Here are the answers to this quiz. Check to see if you made the right connections! Test yourself again on the ones you missed.

1)	h	6)	g	11)	n
2)	c	7)	i	12)	a
3)	d	8)	k	13)	b
4)	e	9)	l	14)	o
5)	f	10)	m	15)	j

Is Erik Erudite or Ethnocentric?

ERSATZ adj. (ERR-SATS) an inferior substitute

Michael sipped a cup of *ersatz* coffee, pursed his lips in distaste, and marveled at his ability to live such a spartan life.

ERUDITE adj. (AIR-YOU-DITE) scholarly, deeply learned, well read

His books were his only extravagance, and while he knew he struck others as *erudite*, he considered himself woefully uninformed.

ESPY v. (ES-PIE) to glimpse, to descry, to catch sight of

One day Michael *espied* a former teacher wandering through an arbor, and drawn to the gaunt figure, began to follow him.

ETHNOCENTRIC adj. the belief in the superiority of one's race or ethnic group

The teacher, Erik Eliason, had been somewhat *ethnocentric* in his thinking, intimating more than once that those students born in his homeland were clearly the most intellectually gifted.

EVANESCENT adj. (EV-UH-NES-ENT) vanishing, happening for the briefest moment

Michael's sighting of Erik however was *evanescent*, for seconds later he seemed to disappear into thin air.

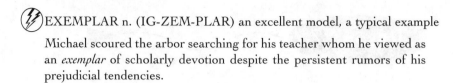

⚡EXEMPLAR n. (IG-ZEM-PLAR) an excellent model, a typical example

Michael scoured the arbor searching for his teacher whom he viewed as an *exemplar* of scholarly devotion despite the persistent rumors of his prejudicial tendencies.

⚡EXIGENT adj. urgent, demands prompt action

Michael felt an *exigent* need to find Erik and express his admiration.

It was not, he knew, an *exigency* (n.), but still, he devoted the following week to tracking down Erik Eliason.

⚡EXTIRPATE v. (EX-TUR-PATE) to rip up by the roots, to abolish, to annihilate

He was so single-minded in his pursuit that he almost *extirpated* the underpinnings of his own life, forgetting to audit classes, read tomes, and meditate on life's most difficult conundrums.

⚡FACETIOUS adj. (FA-SEE-SHUS) humorous, joking in a somewhat inappropriate or clumsy manner

Michael's friend Jim was given to *facetious* remarks whenever confronted with an upsetting situation.

After watching Michael knock on one hundred doors, he commented *facetiously* (adv.), "You know, if you keep this up you might wake up once morning to discover you've become either a travel agent or gumshoe detective instead of a scholar."

FAUNA n. (FAWN-A) animals

Upset at this remark, Michael bolted from the building, and sprinted into the park where he tried to enjoy the exotic *fauna* that meandered freely through the brush.

FECKLESS adj. lacking responsibility, ineffective

Michael realized his *feckless* pursuit of Erik Eliason had undermined his own goals in life and hated himself for it.

⚡FECUND adj. fertile, productive, fruitful

Michael knew he was blessed with a *fecund* mind and that he was wasting it.

His *fecundity* (n.) was an admirable trait, and he was proud of his ability to utilize this gift.

FERAL adj. (FER-UL) wild, like a wild animal, savage

Michael never did detect the true *feral* nature of Erik Eliason who had struck fear into many a student's heart.

FETTER v. to impede, restrain, hamper

Michael was too *fettered* by his own fantasies about the man to allow the rumors of Erik Eliason's vicious temper and prejudices to enter his consciousness.

FEY adj. (FAY) otherworldly, magical, "touched"

Michael went back to his studies, but due to his frightening proclivity for fruitless, single-minded missions, he gained a reputation for being quite *fey*, though in a well-read kind of way.

Plug In

Plug in your answers to see if you've made the right connections. Match the words with their definitions.

__ 1. ERSATZ	(a) productive
__ 2. EVANESCENT	(b) urgent
__ 3. EXIGENT	(c) humorous
__ 4. FECUND	(d) scholarly
__ 5. ETHNOCENTRIC	(e) an imitation
__ 6. FEY	(f) a model
__ 7. FETTER	(g) to glimpse
__ 8. FAUNA	(h) animal
__ 9. FECKLESS	(i) believes in one race's superiority
__ 10. ESPY	(j) to restrain
__ 11. FACETIOUS	(k) irresponsible
__ 12. FERAL	(l) fading
__ 13. EXTIRPATE	(m) to root out
__ 14. EXEMPLAR	(n) a little mad
__ 15. ERUDITE	(o) wild by nature

☼·*Recharge*

Here are the answers to this quiz. Check to see if you made the right connections!

1) 3	6) n	11) c
2) l	7) j	12) o
3) b	8) h	13) m
4) a	9) k	14) f
5) i	10) g	15) d

lesson 28

The Garrulous Gamin
Also Gesticulated!

FLAGELLATE v. to whip, or to punish as if by whipping

Marianne *flagellated* herself for leaving the precious jewel in such a vulnerable location.

The prisoner was sentenced to *flagellation* (n.) for allegedly stealing the purple diamond.

FOMENT v. to stir up, to incite

His imprisonment and punishment *fomented* resentment among the starving lower class to which he belonged.

There was a general *fomentation* (n.) of discontent upon his conviction.

FORSWEAR v. retract, renounce or recant

The judge, who had his doubts as to the prisoner's guilt, would not *forswear* his decision, for fear of looking weak and indecisive.

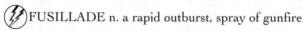FUSILLADE n. a rapid outburst, spray of gunfire

A guard at the prison reported a *fusillade* of gunfire somewhere in the bowels of the building.

The warden received a *fusillade* of written protests from the population at large.

GAINSAY v. to deny, to speak or act against

He invited the *gainsayers* (n.) to write an impassioned letter to the General stating their objections.

GAMIN n. a street urchin, a slim girl with an impish charm

One protestor, a *gamin*, did capture the warden's attention, as she appeared at his door with a sweet smile and a needy, childlike affect.

 GARRULOUS adj. talkative

She proved to be quite *garrulous*, regaling the warden with stories of her pathetic youth and her personal relationship with the prisoner who had been like a father to her.

GERRYMANDER v. to divide into election districts to gain political advantage

The general, feeling the need to bow under pressure, held a vote as to the prisoner's fate, but he *gerrymandered* the state so as to secure the desired outcome.

GESTALT n. a structure, whose parts cannot stand alone

The general did not understand the *gestalt* of the situation, mistakenly believing that a simple rigged election would resolve the conflict.

GESTICULATE v. to gesture, especially when speaking

The gamin returned several times, *gesticulating* wildly to underscore her points, as she tried to convince the warden to sway the general.

GIRD v. to invest with authority, to brace

The warden decided to *gird* himself against an onslaught of the masses, by arming his guards with all manner of weapons.

HABEAS CORPUS n. an order for a prisoner to stand before a judge to determine the legality of his sentence

The prisoner, aware of the writ of *habeas corpus*, and knowing the warden was getting really scared, managed to secure an audience with the judge.

HALITOSIS n. bad breath

The prisoner stood as far away as possible from the judge, as the austere gentlemen suffered from acute *halitosis*.

HIDEBOUND adj. excessively rigid, dry and stiff, inflexible

The *hidebound* judge was clearly finding it difficult to determine the legality of the prisoner's draconian sentence as he never liked to change a decision once he made it.

HISTRIONIC adj. overly dramatic, theatrical, deliberately affected

The prisoner gave forth with such *histrionic* arguments, however, that the judge finally gave in.

His *histrionics* (n.) were so effective that Marianne allowed him to keep the diamond!

Plug In

Plug in your answers to see if you've made the right connections.
Which sentences correctly use the above words?

1. Latitia decided to flagellate herself for completing the physics course, and promptly bought herself a new coat.
   CORRECT   INCORRECT

2. Jacqueline did not want the bad feelings between herself and Dana to foment and so she called to straighten out the misunderstanding.
   CORRECT   INCORRECT

3. While James could not forswear his statement that David cheated, he recanted the accusation.
   CORRECT   INCORRECT

4. There was just the smallest fusillade of resentment when Karen stole the show.
   CORRECT   INCORRECT

5. The gainsayer could not have agreed more.
   CORRECT   INCORRECT

6. When Reshmi answered the door a gamin stood before her looking as fierce and street smart as any gang member possibly could.
   CORRECT   INCORRECT

7. Five-year-old Dao was so garrulous that his mother actually let him watch television just to shut him up.
        CORRECT   INCORRECT

8. The democrats gerrymandered the county in order to pass their programs on election day.
        CORRECT   INCORRECT

9. "It's the gestalt of the thing," Jason tried to explain when the lawyer continually focussed only on the absence of motive.
        CORRECT   INCORRECT

10. Gerry gesticulated broadly as he spoke which unfortunately drew attention away from his words.
        CORRECT   INCORRECT

11. Sara girded herself for the fury of her disappointed and resentful fifteen-year-old.
        CORRECT   INCORRECT

12. The writ of habeas corpus was disallowed in the principality, and so Maurice was able to challenge his sentence.
        CORRECT   INCORRECT

13. Jeannette's halitosis was not only charming but quite alluring too.
        CORRECT   INCORRECT

14. The teacher was so hidebound that the students were allowed to hand in papers whenever they got the chance.
        CORRECT   INCORRECT

15. The president's histrionics made him look less like a president and more like a petulant child.
        CORRECT   INCORRECT

The answer key appears on the following page.

⋰۞⋱*Recharge*

Here are the answers to this quiz. Check to see if you made the right connections! Test yourself again on the ones you missed.

1. incorrect	6. incorrect	11. correct
2. correct	7. correct	12. incorrect
3. incorrect	8. correct	13. incorrect
4. incorrect	9. correct	14. incorrect
5. incorrect	10. correct	15. correct

Can Homeopathy Cure an Ignominious Past?

HOARY adj. (HORE-EE) gray or white with age, ancient, stale

The old man's *hoary* beard and glazed eyes created a dramatic picture.

His *hoary* abode was covered with dust and old dirty clothes and plates.

HOMEOPATHY n. a system of natural healing

He had clearly dabbled in *homeopathy* as there were books on the subject everywhere.

The shelves was filled with *homeopathic* (adj.) medications.

HUSBANDRY n. the judicious used of resources, livestock farming

He clearly practiced *husbandry* but he was hardly as destitute as his living arrangements seemed to indicate.

The old man had *husbanded* (v.) his money, for though he lived like a hermit his bank account was overflowing.

IGNOMINIOUS adj. disgraceful and dishonorable

The old man spoke to no one for years as he was dreadfully ashamed of his *ignominious* past.

He had, in his younger days, accepted a bribe to stay quiet about a vicious crime, and after he got out of jail, he sentenced himself to a life of *ignominy* (n.).

IMBROGLIO n. (IM-BROLE-YO) a difficult and confused situation, a complicated disagreement

He was driven to accept the bribe because of a heated *imbroglio* in his own life which left him no choice but to act unethically.

IMPECUNIOUS adj. without money, penniless

After serving a sentence, the old man chose to live as if he were *impecunious*, as a sort of ongoing penance for his mistake.

IMPERVIOUS adj. does not allow something to pass through, impenetrable

He seemed *impervious* to the advertisements for luxurious trappings he could have well afforded.

IMPUGN v. (IM-PUNE) to attack the integrity of something

The old man knew his was not the only reputation that was *impugned* by the events, as there were others who also accepted bribes.

IMPLACABLE adj. not capable of being appeased or mollified

He had remained *implacable*, even after his sentence was over, lying awake at night riddled with regrets.

INCHOATE adj. (IN-CO-UT) just beginning, not organized or orderly, incomplete

However, now that he was near death the old man had an *inchoate* sense that perhaps he'd punished himself too severely.

INIQUITOUS adj. evil, unjust

He had indeed committed an *iniquitous* act, but perhaps enough, should have been enough.

It was an act of *iniquity* (n.), but it was done and over.

INSOUCIANT adj. (IN-SOO-SEE-ENT) nonchalant, lighthearted, unconcerned

The old man had noticed that the others who had also lied had gone on, after their sentences were commuted, to lead pleasant, *insouciant* lives.

INTERREGNUM n. the period between two successive governments, a pause in a continuing series

There was a brief time, during the *interregnum*, directly after King Ricardo had died and King Stag began his reign that all criminals were forgiven.

INTRANSIGENT adj. uncompromising, stubborn

King Stag was an *intransigent* sort and unlikely to commute the sentence of anyone.

INVETERATE adj. habitual, deeply rooted or established

The old man had understood this about King Stag, but being an *inveterate* masochist, he had opted to finish his sentence anyway; now, upon his deathbed, he regretted it.

Plug In

Plug in your answers to see if you've made the right connections. Pick the correct definition.

1) HOARY
   a) evil
   b) ancient
   c) cheap

2) HOMEOPATHY
   a) study of man
   b) system of natural medicine
   c) study of families

3) HUSBANDRY
   a) thrifty
   b) marriage minded
   c) cheap

4) IGNOMINIOUS
   a) complicated
   b) disgraceful
   c) unintelligent

5) IMBROGLIO
   a) a puzzle
   b) a difficult situation
   c) a fight

6) IMPECUNIOUS
   a) habitual
   b) nonchalant
   c) penniless

7) IMPERVIOUS
   a) superior
   b) rude
   c) impenetrable

8) IMPLACABLE
   a) unusually impatient
   b) orderly
   c) can't be appeased

9) IMPUGN
   a) punish
   b) imprison
   c) attack

10) INCHOATE
    a) just beginning
    b) incomprehensible
    c) uncompromising

11) INIQUITOUS
    a) unequal
    b) unjust
    c) unusual

12) INSOUCIANT
    a) silly
    b) immature
    c) nonchalant

13) INTERREGNUM
   a) dishonorable
   b) between two governments
   c) in the middle

14) INTRANSIGENT
   a) on the road
   b) stubborn
   c) unjust

15) INVETERATE
   a) under attack
   b) dishonorable
   c) habitual

Recharge

Here are the answers to this quiz. Check to see if you made the right connections! Test yourself again on the ones you missed.

1.	b	6.	c	11.	b
2.	b	7.	c	12.	c
3.	a	8.	c	13.	b
4.	b	9.	c	14.	b
5.	b	10.	a	15.	c

lesson 30

Libidinous Libations or Military Machinations?

IRASCIBLE adj. (IR-RAS-UH-BULL) hot-tempered, cranky

General Wrath was known for his *irascible* nature and so most army personnel steered clear of him as much as possible.

His *irascibility* (n.) was known throughout the ranks.

ITINERANT adj. moving from place to place

Many blamed his explosive personality on his *itinerant* childhood, which afforded him little opportunity to settled down and connect well with others.

JUGGERNAUT n. a massive, unstoppable object

The *juggernaut* of war was the thing that centered and inspired General Wrath.

JUNTA n. (HOON-TUH) a small group that rules a country after a coup d'etat

Secretly, he was thrilled that a vicious *junta* had taken over the country of Qiala, as it afforded him an opportunity to take up arms.

LARGESS n. a generous giving of gifts, philanthropy

The junta attempted to hide their ill intent by extending considerable and immediate *largess* towards the common folk.

LASSITUDE n. a weariness, listlessness, a state of lethargy

The army had fallen into a sort of *lassitude* that the General abhorred and was more than happy to erase.

LEITMOTIF n. (LITE-MOTEEF) a dominant or recurring theme

The General marched into the barracks one morning and boomed, "We will search out and punish all lazy bums starting today," and indeed this proved to be his *leitmotif* throughout the war.

LEVEE n. an embankment designed to prevent a river from flooding

Unfortunately some of his men were called away on a national emergency to help build a *levee* along the Mississippi River.

LIBATION n. a pouring of a liquid for a religious ceremony, a drink

Those soldiers chosen to build the levee drank a *libation* to the mysterious powers of fate, which had kept them from the violent front.

LIBIDINOUS adj. lustful, lascivious

They also drank a libation to the goddess of love in the hopes that they would soon be able to realize their *libidinous* fantasies.

LOPE v. to run at steady, easy pace

After completing the levee the soldiers gleefully *loped* to the nearest saloon, where, officially off duty, they guzzled a few beers.

MACERATE v. MASS-ER-ATE to soften by soaking, to cause to waste away

They did however, feel significant guilt for their captured comrades who were *macerating* in the prisons of Qiala.

MACHINATION n. (MASH-IN-A-TION) scheming activity for an evil purpose

The ruthless *machinations* of the junta were proving to be too much for the General's sturdy but small army.

⚡MALAPROPISM n. the humorous misuse of a word that sounds very much like the word intended.

"There's a whore out there?!" exclaimed an old, partially deaf man when told to vacate his home because of the "war out there." "That's a *malapropism*," the junta peon informed him.

MALFEASANCE n. (MAL-FEE-SUNS) an illegal act especially by a public official

The General had to retreat, by order of the president who, though under investigation for a *malfeasance*, was always empowered to bring the men home.

Plug In

Plug in your answers to see if you've made the right connections.
Fill in the blanks using the words below.

(a) irascible	(f) lassitude	(k) lope
(b) itinerant	(g) leitmotif	(l) macerate
(c) juggernaut	(h) levee	(m) machination
(d) junta	(i) libation	(n) malapropism
(e) largess	(j) libidinous	(o) malfeasance

1. Rashanda gracefully _____ across the softball field.

2. Chef Matsuri attempted to _____ the herbs in a cup of water.

3. Tom Joad, the migrant worker, was tired of his _____ life and wished to finally settle down.

4. The _____ of the evil wizard were beyond anyone's worse nightmares.

5. Gabriel drank a _____ to his guardian angel who he believed had saved the day.

6. The _____ had simply declared themselves in charge and initiated land reform.

7. She could be _____ when spoken to rudely.

8. When faced with the _____ of protesting truck drivers, the union gave in.

9. Ms. Steinem's _____ was especially welcomed by the young, single mother who had no place else to run.

10. It is a _____ to say, "What a feather in your lap!"

11. The president's _____ ruined his place in history.

12. James Allen was given to _____ daydreams, which while exciting, were a little too lecherous to share with anyone.

13. After days of running a fever, Adam fell into a state of complete _____.

14. The singer used as his _____ a martini glass filled with colored water, and during every performance joked of his love of liquor.

15. The _____ did not hold and so the river flooded the terrain.

⌁ Recharge

Here are the answers to this quiz. Check to see if you made the right connections! Test yourself again on the ones you missed.

1) k	6) d	11) o
2) l	7) a	12) j
3) b	8) c	13) f
4) m	9) e	14) g
5) i	10) n	15) h

lesson 31

A Mirthful or Miasmic Milieu?

MARTINET n. one who adheres strictly to rules

There were so many rules, so strictly followed by so many, that Mai began to feel as if her office was staffed by *martinets*.

MATRICULATE v. to enroll, most particularly in college

She began to wonder if she should have *matriculated* at the local university instead of taking a year off to experience the "real world."

MAUDLIN adj. (MAWD-LIN) overly sentimental

Mai's mother had displayed such a *maudlin* concern for her daughter's academic future that Mai wanted to suggest that her mother matriculate as well.

MELLIFLUOUS adj. (MEL-LI-FLU-OUS) sweetly flowing

Instead, Mai used *mellifluous* language to get her mother to agree to allow her to take the year off.

MENDACIOUS adj. (MEN-DAY-SHUS) dishonest, deceitful

Actually Mai felt a bit *mendacious*, as she wasn't at all sure she did want to attend college and was using the "year off" strategy as a ploy.

Mai's *mendacity* (n.) was not something of which she was proud.

MERCURIAL adj.(MER-CURE-EE-UL) emotionally unpredictable, give to rapid changes in mood

Mai realized this wasn't wise, for her mother had a *mercurial* personality and if she believed herself deceived, she might refuse Mai any financial assistance during her year off.

MIASMA n. (MY-AZ-MA) a poisonous swamp vapor, a harmful influence or atmosphere

Now that Mai was at the office, she felt as if she were in a *miasma* of brainwashed cadets.

MILIEU n. (MILL-YOO) environment, surroundings

Mai began to wonder if college were not the more appropriate *milieu* for someone like herself.

MIRTHFUL n. merry, gleeful

She began to long for the *mirthful* camaraderie her college friends enjoyed.

⚡MORDANT adj. bitingly sarcastic, incisive, caustic in manner

Mai was also hurt by their *mordant* tone when teasing her about her choice.

⚡MORIBUND adj. being in a dying or decaying condition

Mai grew *moribund*, as she weathered the last months of her commitment to the workplace.

MUCKRAKE v. to expose political misconduct

Things did get a bit more interesting in the office for a short while, when one of the workers dabbled in a little *muckraking* to make sure the mayor was not re-elected.

⚡MUNIFICENT adj. generous

At Christmas time, Mai's pain was lessened somewhat by the generous bonus offered by her *munificent* boss.

MYOPIA n. nearsightedness, lacking foresight

Mai was convinced that his *myopia* would eventually run the business into the ground—he seemed incapable of responding to new trends in fashion.

His *myopic* (adj) tendencies were unfortunate.

NABOB n. (NAY-BOB) a wealthy, influential person

Mai could not understand how he had become such a *nabob* in the industry when she was sure he had a limited IQ and was served by an office of poorly dressed robots.

Plug In

Plug in your answers to see if you've made the right connections.
Match the word to its closest opposite:

__ 1. MARTINET	(a) support a politician
__ 2. MATRICULATE	(b) drop out
__ 3. MAUDLIN	(c) flexible person
__ 4. MELLIFLUOUS	(d) joyless
__ 5. MENDACIOUS	(e) honest
__ 6. MERCURIAL	(f) gently phrased
__ 7. MIASMA	(g) unsentimental
__ 8. MILIEU	(h) healthy atmosphere
__ 9. MIRTHFUL	(i) farsightedness
__ 10. MORDANT	(j) stingy
__ 11. MORIBUND	(k) hard to listen to
__ 12. MUCKRAKE	(l) a poor nobody
__ 13. MUNIFICENT	(m) full of life
__ 14. MYOPIA	(n) even-tempered
__ 15. NABOB	(o) exact spot

🔆Recharge

Here are the answers to this quiz. Check to see if you made the right connections! Test yourself again on the ones you missed.

1. c	6. n	11. m
2. b	7. h	12. a
3. g	8. o	13. j
4. k	9. d	14. i
5. e	10. f	15. l

Is Natalie the Nonplussed Neophyte?

NASCENT adj. coming into existence, being born

The concept for the advertising campaign was yet in the *nascent* stage.

The *nascence* (n.) of the advertising campaign was being watched and assessed by everyone.

NEOPHYTE n. a beginner, a novice

Natalie, a *neophyte* on the account, was quite nervous over the attention, as she was sure her inexperience would shine forth like a beacon.

NEPOTISM n. showing favoritism to friends or family, as in granting positions in jobs or politics

She knew she'd landed on the account as a result of *nepotism,* because her uncle was the creative director.

NIGGARDLY adj. stingy, small in a mean way

Natalie, had so far received only *niggardly* praise from Robert, her insecure superior, who was clearly annoyed by her skills.

NIHILISM n. the belief that there are no values or morals in the universe, that existence is senseless or useless

Robert held *nihilism* as a basic truth of life and was rarely positive towards anyone or anything.

His *nihilistic* (adj.) views often brought everybody down.

NIRVANA n. a blissful, painless state, a supreme happiness according to Buddhism when the soul is no longer in need of purification of hatred, deceit, etc.

Natalie, on the other hand, fully intended and expected to experience some moments of pure *nirvana* in her life, and so she remained undaunted by her boss's attitude.

NOISOME adj. harmful, unwholesome, stinking, putrid

Natalie only wished that the product they were pitching, *Fliss*, did not have such a *noisome* aspect, as it was difficult to support a loathsome cleaning fluid.

NONPLUS v. to bewilder, to puzzle

Natalie was quite *nonplussed* when Robert announced one morning that the ad campaign for *Fliss* should tell it like it is—warts and all.

OBDURATE adj. stubborn

Sasha, the creative director, however, was *obdurate* in her position that outlining the negatives was no way to make a consumer trust a product.

OBSEQUIOUS adj. fawning, subservient, servile

Robert immediately lost his commitment to the negative as an angle, and became *obsequious* in his admiration for the director's perspective.

OEUVRE n. (OO-VER) a work of art, the sum of an artist's work

The truth was the creative director had an impressive *oeuvre* that spanned twenty years of creative ad campaigns.

OFFICIOUS adj. unnecessarily helpful, meddlesome, interfering

The director's new and *officious* assistant bustled in and out of the room during this key meeting, bothering everyone with unwanted comments and overall intrusiveness.

OMNISCIENT adj. all knowing, infinite awareness

Everyone grew quiet when the president of the firm entered the conference room, as he was thought to be utterly *omniscient* in his knowledge of the business.

OMNIVOROUS adj. eating or absorbing everything, feeding on both animal and vegetable substances

Natalie was *omnivorous* when it came to learning what she could of the business, and so she hung on the president's every word.

ONEROUS adj. burdensome, oppressive, troublesome

Things grew *onerous* immediately however, as the president had come to announce his intention to dismiss them all if a terrific new campaign was not forthcoming . . . a move that only served to support Robert's nihilistic views and alert Natalie to the fact that a state of nirvana was not imminent.

Plug In

Plug in your answers to see if you've made the right connections. Choose the correct definition for each word.

1. NASCENT
    a) young
    b) being born
    c) meddlesome

2. NEOPHYTE
    a) inexperienced
    b) immature
    c) unknowledgeable

3. NEPOTISM
    a) a blissful state
    b) a belief in the uselessness of it all
    c) using favoritism for advancement

4. NIGGARDLY
    a) stingy
    b) slow
    c) bewildering

5 .NIHILISM
    a) useless of it all
    b) nature's fury
    c) the afterlife

6. NIRVANA
   a) a work of art
   b) a beginner
   c) a state of bliss

7. NOISOME
   a) putrid
   b) noisy
   c) oppressive

8. NONPLUS
   a) perplex
   b) horrify
   c) relieve

9. OBDURATE
   a) solid as an object
   b) long in duration
   c) stubborn

10. OBSEQUIOUS
    a) obnoxious
    b) groveling
    c) sequential

11. OEUVRE
    a) work in progress
    b) an artist's lifetime portfolio
    c) an open door

12. OFFICIOUS
    a) formal
    b) unnecessarily and overly involved
    c) official

13. OMNISCIENT
    a) all knowing
    b) everywhere
    c) just beginning

14) OMNIVOROUS
   a)   take in everything
   b)   meat eater
   c)   meddlesome

15) ONEROUS
   a)   the generosity of one
   b)   confusing
   c)   oppressive

☀ *Recharge*

Here are the answers to this quiz. Check to see if you made the right connections! Test yourself again on the ones you missed.

1.	b	6.	c	11.	b
2.	a	7.	a	12.	b
3.	c	8.	a	13.	a
4.	a	9.	c	14.	a
5.	a	10.	b	15.	c

Is the Panegyric an Opus in Patois?

ONUS n. burden, blame, obligation

The lawyer had miscalculated the skills of his opponent, and so the *onus* was on him to somehow save the case.

OPPROBRIOUS adj. damning, extremely critical, disgraceful

The defendant had absolutely committed the crime, but fancy footwork had allowed *opprobrious* evidence to lose its significance.

The prosecutor felt he would bring *opprobrium* (n.) upon himself if he failed to win the case.

OPUS n. a creative work, musical composition

The prosecutor wished to consider his work on the case an *opus* in fine lawyering.

One juror was in a particular hurry to reach a verdict as she was in the middle of writing an *opus* and was afraid she'd lose her inspiration.

OSCILLATE v. to swing back and forth

The fans, *oscillating* in the ceiling, did very little to cool off the hot tempers in the courtroom.

OSSIFY v. to become rigid, to be come set in one's ways

The judge, somewhat *ossified* by the courtroom dramatics, was becoming more and more annoyed by the attorneys' clear plays for sympathy.

⚡ PALLIATE v. to hide the seriousness of something with excuses or apologies, to ease without curing

The crime was so vicious, it seemed useless to try to *palliate* what had happened that night.

The lawyer took an aspirin as a *palliative* (n.) in the hopes that he might regain his composure.

⚡ PALLID adj. lacking color, wan

The defendant grew *pallid* when pictures of the crime he allegedly committed were displayed to the jury.

PANACEA n. (PAN-A-SEE-A) a remedy that cures everything

It was obvious to everyone there was no *panacea* on Earth that could ease the pain of the victims' relatives.

⚡ PANEGYRIC n. (PAN-E-JIR-IC) lofty praise, eulogistic writing

The prosecutor launched in a *panegyric,* citing the victim's good works and close, meaningful, personal relationships.

PARADIGM n. (PAR-A-DIME) a model or example

Using an earlier case as a *paradigm,* the prosecutor attempted to concentrate on two pieces of key evidence, instead of a wider array that might have confused the jury.

⚡ PARSIMONIOUS adj. stingy

One juror, a particularly *parsimonious* woman, noticed that the defendant's attorney, wore very expensive suits and ties.

PATINA n. surface discoloration caused by age and oxidation, a superficial covering or exterior

She also noticed the lovely *patina* on the antique tables behind which the attorneys sat.

PATOIS n. (PA-TWA) a language used by a particular population that differs from standard speech

This juror was also extremely taken by the defendant's *patois,* which she struggled to understand even while she admired its lilt.

PENULTIMATE adj. next to last

The lawyer's *penultimate* remarks were clearly meant to grab the jurors' attention.

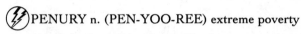PENURY n. (PEN-YOO-REE) extreme poverty

The defendant claimed to suffer from *penury,* but it was clear from the attire of his attorneys that this was highly unlikely, and so the jury were loathe to offer him much sympathy—or an acquittal.

Plug In

Plug in your answers to see if you've made the right connections.
Match the word with its correct definition.

__ 1.	ONUS	(a)	stinginess
__ 2.	OPPROBRIOUS	(b)	surface discoloration
__ 3.	OPUS	(c)	to swing back and forth
__ 4.	OSCILLATE	(d)	high praise
__ 5.	OSSIFY	(e)	to become rigid
__ 6.	PALLIATE	(f)	extreme poverty
__ 7.	PALLID	(g)	next to last
__ 8.	PANACEA	(h)	burden
__ 9.	PANEGYRIC	(i)	a creative work
__ 10.	PARADIGM	(j)	a model
__ 11.	PARSIMONY	(k)	a cure for everything
__ 12.	PATINA	(l)	critical
__ 13.	PATOIS	(m)	a variation on standard language
__ 14.	PENULTIMATE	(n)	lacking color
__ 15.	PENURY	(o)	to ease

☀Recharge

Here are the answers to this quiz. Check to see if you made the right connections! Test yourself again on the ones you missed.

1. h	6. o	11. a
2. l	7. n	12. b
3. i	8. k	13. m
4. c	9. d	14. g
5. e	10. j	15. f

A Perfidious or Phlegmatic Plebeian?

PEREGRINATION n. an expedition, wandering

Little Megan's *peregrinations* around the perimeter of the nursery school classroom were filled with discovery.

PERFIDIOUS adj. faithless, untrustworthy

Unfortunately when Megan was not at the school she was in the hands of a *perfidious* baby-sitter, who frequently left her charge unattended.

The sitter's *perfidy* (n) was unforgivable.

PERFUNCTORY adj. careless, unenthusiastic, done merely as duty

She would, in a *perfunctory* manner, make Megan lunch, park her in front of the TV, and then salivate over the phone with her latest boyfriend.

PERORATE v. to make a long, formal speech, to sum up a speech

Once a year the nursery school director would *perorate* on the subject of good childcare, but she could tell most parents believed they already had the issue well under control.

After delivering her talk she would *perorate* with some dramatic warnings, but no one ever took heed.

Her *peroration* (n.) was meant to grab the attention of her audience, but they were a restless, inattentive group, and so her words fell on deaf ears.

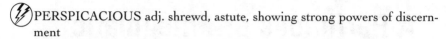

PERQUISITE n. a privilege or perk that goes along with a job

There were not many *perquisites* available to the teachers at the nursery school, and so to keep her staff happy, the director often treated them to sumptuous dinners.

PERSPICACIOUS adj. shrewd, astute, showing strong powers of discernment

Megan was fortunately quite *perspicacious;* realizing her sitter was basically ineffectual, she learned to entertain and care for herself.

PETULANT adj. cranky, ill tempered, irritable, peevish

She might have been more *petulant,* as is the typical nature of a four-year-old, except that she sensed the sitter would not have noticed.

PHANTASM n. an apparition, phantom

In fact, the sitter was haunted by such *phantasms* of insecurity that she thought of no one but herself.

Her *phantasmal* (adj.) fears came and went with no warning.

She had an alarming *phantasmagorical* (adj.) inner life, filled with a kind of carousel of visions and anxieties.

PHILISTINE n. a smugly insensitive and ignorant person who has no knowledge of intellectual or artistic subjects

Megan believed her sitter to be a *philistine*, especially when it came to the fine art of finger painting.

PHLEGMATIC adj. calm, indifferent, not easily aroused

"You're dumb," Megan once snapped at her when she could no longer contain her frustration, but the sitter received the criticism with a *phlegmatic,* "Yes. I'm dumb."

PIQUANT adj. pungent, charmingly provocative

Megan had a certain *piquant* quality, and as a result charmed all who were in her presence, except perhaps, the sitter.

Her *piquancy* (n.) was noted early on, with great admiration, by all the relatives.

PLACEBO n. a fake medication

> Megan, for some unfathomable reason, liked to fake illness, and so her parents would administer a *placebo* such as a tiny, round, sweet, candy in order to make the "tummy ache" go away.

PLEBEIAN n. common, vulgar, low class

> When they discovered that the sitter's method of coping with Megan's "illnesses" was to give her huge candy bars, popcorn, and a thriller on video, they concluded she was a *plebeian*.

PLURALISM n. a society in which distinct groups function together, but retain their identities

> The sitter, enraged by her boss's snobbery, delivered a diatribe on *pluralism,* pointing out that though she'd been brought up on the wrong side of the tracks, she was still able to care for Megan.
>
> "In a *pluralistic* (adj.) society, people learn to live together," she continued loftily.

PORTENT n. an omen, a sign of something coming, a foreshadowing

> Still, Megan's parents considered the sitter's reaction to the child's "illness" a *portent* of worse judgment calls, and so they fired her. This left them with no child care to support the lifestyle to which they hoped to remain accustomed.

Plug In

Plug in your answers to see if you've made the right connections.
Which of the following sentences are correct?

1. Rashad's peregrination to the grocery store took only five minutes.
    CORRECT   INCORRECT

2. The dean was so perfidious that he could countenance not a single criticism of his staff if it was not entirely well founded.
    CORRECT   INCORRECT

3. Jamie gave a perfunctory speech that inspired little applause.
    CORRECT   INCORRECT

4. Mrs. Wellstone perorated on the subject of child abuse to an audience of political movers and shakers, hoping to inspire some new legislation.
    CORRECT   INCORRECT

5. A perquisite to enrolling in a fine college, is good grades.
    CORRECT   INCORRECT

6. Mr. Nguyen, a perspicacious man, typically hadn't a clue about what Mrs. Nguyen was really trying to convey.
    CORRECT   INCORRECT

7. Ron displayed his petulance by stamping his foot and screaming at the top of his lungs.
    CORRECT   INCORRECT

8. The sudden appearance of a stream running through the barren land was only a phantasm, born of the farmer's distress.
    CORRECT   INCORRECT

9. "You are truly a philistine," the professor exclaimed, proudly handing her favorite student a diploma.
    CORRECT   INCORRECT

10. The Queen's phlegmatic attitude towards the masses proved to be her downfall.
    CORRECT   INCORRECT

11. She looked so piquant, the swim coach knew immediately she would win every race.
    CORRECT   INCORRECT

12. Jamal gave his son a placebo hoping it was all that was needed to rid the child of his headaches.
    CORRECT   INCORRECT

13. Andre was a true plebeian, having been educated in the finest schools around the world.
    CORRECT   INCORRECT

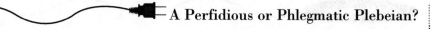

14. Melissa was intrigued by the concept of pluralism which seemed to underline the impossibility of different groups existing comfortably together.
          CORRECT   INCORRECT

15. The dark clouds portended a vicious storm.
          CORRECT   INCORRECT

☀Recharge

Here are the answers to this quiz. Check to see if you made the right connections! Test yourself again on the ones you missed.

1.	incorrect	6.	incorrect	11.	incorrect
2.	incorrect	7.	correct	12.	correct
3.	correct	8.	correct	13.	incorrect
4.	correct	9.	incorrect	14.	correct
5.	incorrect	10.	correct	15.	correct

Is Protean Paulo Also Punctilious?

PREGNANT adj. highly significant, overflowing, rich in significance

There was a *pregnant* pause in the room when Paulo announced his intention to close his business and take off to see the world.

PREPOSSESS v. to cause to be preoccupied, to influence, positively, in advance

Paulo had been, he admitted, *prepossessed* by thoughts of wandering freely through countrysides and ocean shores.

He had always been a *prepossessing* (adj.) sort, and imagined this time too, people would embrace his notion.

PRESCIENT adj. having foresight

"You are not being particularly *prescient* in this decision," Paulo's best friend Carlos commented, "as you could come back a pauper."

PREVARICATE v. to deviate from the truth

"I do no wish to *prevaricate*," Paulo replied, "as the simple truth is, your worries are not mine and I must follow my own heart."

"Are you sure that is not a *prevarication* (n.)," his other friend queried, "for perhaps you are really just upset by the down turn in profits you have been experiencing."

PRIVATION n. lack of comforts, poverty, a state of being deprived

"You have never suffered from *privation*," Abby, his girlfriend warned, "and I wonder how you would manage if such a state came to pass."

PROBITY n. honesty, uprightness

"I can say with complete *probity*, that I could manage with very little," Paulo responded confidently.

⚡ PROFLIGATE adj. corrupt, degenerate, wildly extravagant

"I have never," he continued, "been a *profligate* spender — material things have always meant little to me."

"I hope, during the course of my journey, to fight *profligate* activity everywhere."

⚡ PROPINQUITY adj. nearness in place or time, kinship

"Our *propinquity* to each other will make the coming separation quite difficult," Paulo noted gently.

⚡ PROTEAN adj. readily assuming different shapes or characters

"You have always exhibited a *protean* quality," Abby sighed, "one day a jester, the next an academician, and now a nomad."

PROVENANCE n. origin, source, proof of past ownership

"Was the *provenance* of your plans the recent film by the famous director Gustaf?" asked Gabriel, another good friend.

"Before you go will you be providing me with the *provenance* of that painting you wish me to sell?" asked Abby.

PROWESS n. exceptional skill or strength, military valor

"My ideas are my own," Paulo assured the crowd of friends, "and I intend to seek my fortune with all the *prowess* I have brought to my other endeavors."

PRURIENT adj. lascivious, have lustful thoughts or desires

"And what of your *prurient* leanings, which you have so far managed to safely contain under our watchful eyes?" Todd murmured, bringing a blush to Abby's cheeks.

PUISSANCE adj. power, strength

"The *puissance* of my desires can be healthfully contained by my rich fantasy life," Paulo insisted.

PUNCTILIOUS adj. meticulously attentive to detail, exacting

"It amazes me that a *punctilious* fellow like you could possibly think you would enjoy a journey with no specific time or place in . . . mind," chuckled . . . Abraham.

PUTREFY v. to rot

The cheese began to *putrefy* after two days out in the hot sun.

Plug In

Plug in your answers to see if you've made the right connections. Choose the correct definition for each word.

1. PREGNANT
   a) slight
   b) heavy with meaning
   c) confusing

2. PREPOSSESS
   a) to own
   b) to desire
   c) to preoccupy

3. PRESCIENT
   a) ancient
   b) near
   c) having foresight

4. PREVARICATE
   a) to worry
   b) to vacillate
   c) to color the truth

5. PRIVATION
   a) poverty
   b) power
   c) honesty

6. PROBITY
   a) doubt
   b) power
   c) honesty

7. PROFLIGATE
   a) powerful
   b) lustful
   c) corrupt

8. PROPINQUITY
   a) foresight
   b) nearness
   c) expansiveness

9. PROTEAN
   a) makes a good impression
   b) takes on different shapes
   c) lustful

10. PROVENANCE
    a) origin
    b) fate
    c) future

11. PROWESS
    a) forthrightness
    b) skill
    c) bravery

12. PRURIENT
    a) lustful
    b) violent
    c) immature

13. PUISSANT
    a) influence
    b) power
    c) scent

14. PUNCTILIOUS
    a) extravagant
    b) annoying
    c) detail oriented

15. PUTREFY
    a) to anger
    b) to impress
    c) to decay

⚡ Recharge

Here are the answers to this quiz. Check to see if you made the right connections! Test yourself again on the ones you missed.

1.	b	6.	c	11.	b
2.	c	7.	c	12.	a
3.	c	8.	b	13.	b
4.	c	9.	b	14.	c
5.	a	10.	a	15.	c

Is a Raffish and Ribald Repartee Enough?

QUIESCENCE n. (KWEE-ESS-ENSE) state of rest or inactivity

Peter's criminal activity typically fell into a state of *quiescence* during the winter months.

RAFFISH adj. (RAY-FISH) jaunty, sporty, disreputable, vulgar, characterized by a careless unconventionality

Peter exuded a certain *raffish* charm; when not behind bars, he exhibited quite a way with the ladies.

RAPPROCHEMENT n. (RA-PROSH-MON) a re-establishment of good relations

Peter had experienced a serious falling out with his mother, Mary, after he elected to pursue a life of crime and did not expect a *rapprochement* anytime soon.

RAREFIED adj. esoteric, interesting to only a few

Mary hailed from a rather *rarefied* background, having been brought up by nuns close by her father's castle high in the mountains of Luxembourg.

RECALCITRANT adj. stubbornly defiant and resistant of authority

Her son had been an extraordinarily *recalcitrant* toddler who would not give in, even if threatened with a month of no desserts.

His *recalcitrance* (n.) was worse than that of most two-year-olds.

RECIDIVISM n. the act of repeating an offense.

> When it became clear that Peter, as an adult, had become a criminal, she was not lulled by his periods of good behavior, as she knew the chance of *recidivism* was great.

> She assumed her son would be a *recidivist*.

RECONDITE adj. hard to understand, abstruse, over one's head

> She would have delivered a speech on morality to her son, but recognized that to Peter it would have been *recondite*, little more than pig latin.

REDOUBTABLE adj. formidable, fearsome, deserving of respect

> Peter's mother felt she might have been able to show Peter the error of his ways but the *redoubtable* circle in which he traveled minimized her influence over him.

REMUNERATION n. payment, recompense

> "I just don't feel that a career involving hard work is *remuneration* enough for me," Peter spoke up frankly.

> "I want a career that is *remunerative* (adj.) in a material vein."

REPARTEE n. (REP-ARE-TAY) a quick, witty reply, spirited conversation

> Peter, though morally bereft, was quite skilled in *repartee* and could amuse his friends endlessly with his golden tongue.

REPROBATE n. a morally unprincipled person, a scoundrel

> His best friend, Adrian, was a *reprobate* from way back, having committed his first robbery at age ten.

> Adrian received strong *reprobation* (n.) at the time, but the strong disapproval did little to set him straight.

RETICENT adj. (RET-I-SENT) restrained, reluctant, uncommunicative

> Peter's mother had been *reticent* to tell her friends about her son's lifestyle, but now she concluded she had to cut him out of her life.

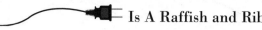

RIBALD adj. (RIB-ULD) vulgar or indecent language

Peter, deeply hurt, greeted his mother's damnation of him with *ribald* humor, which only served to aggravate her considerable hurt and disappointment.

RIFE adj. widespread, abounding, occurring frequently

"Your life is *rife* with degradation and ugliness!" Mary sobbed, with tears pouring down her face.

ROUT v. (ROWT) to put to flight, to scatter, to cause a huge defeat

"The police will *rout* you from your sordid life, and then you'll have no one to come visit you in jail!" she cried out ominously.

Plug In

Plug in your answers to see if you've made the right connections.
Fill in the blanks with the correct words.

(a) quiescence   (f) recidivist   (k) reprobate
(b) raffish   (g) recondite   (l) reticent
(c) rapprochement   (h) redoubtable   (m) ribald
(d) rarefied   (i) remuneration   (n) rife
(e) recalcitrant   (j) repartee   (o) rout

1. After a long feud, Ramon and David were able to achieve a _____, after which they rarely argued.

2. The politician's speech was so utterly _____, he lost the votes of half a town in those fifteen minutes.

3. Hannah was _____ to take the journey as she'd heard it was going to be a rough ride.

4. The organization was _____ with disloyal employees, who systematically wore away at profits.

5. The king's men _____ the thieves from their den and promptly threw them into a dark forbidding dungeon.

6. Stacey was a chronic shoplifter, and though she tried all manner of therapy to help her break the habit, in the eyes of many she was considered a _____.

7. The selection of book in the store was so _____, the shopkeeper sold only one a day, if he was lucky.

8. Armand and his _____ friends often behaved in an unruly, and crude fashion when standing on the street corner.

9. Wanda enjoyed a time of _____ while caring for her newborn quietly at home with the help of an able and energetic nanny.

10. Jason wanted the job of janitor but was not happy with the _____ offered during the interview.

11. The dinner party sparkled with the clever _____ of the guests.

12. Nate's pal had a kind heart, but so many problems, and so much anger, that to think of him as a _____ was rather accurate.

13. Mr. McBride's _____ comments amused some, but offended most.

14. Jan's attachment to her demented girlfriend was so _____ no one dared separate them though clearly the relationship was compromising her health.

15. Fifteen-year-old Dylan remained totally _____ even when confronted with the evidence of his lies.

☀ Recharge

Here are the answers to this quiz. Check to see if you made the right connections! Test yourself again on the ones you missed.

1. c	6. f	11. j
2. g	7. d	12. k
3. l	8. b	13. m
4. n	9. a	14. h
5. o	10. i	15. e

Will Sasha Sally Towards a Sagacious Story?

RUBRIC n. (ROO-BRICK) heading, title, category

Sasha dreamed of one day writing a book that would come under the *rubric* of historical fiction.

RUMINATE v. (ROO-MIN-ATE) to muse upon

She *ruminated* for months about which historical period to use and what historical characters to inspire her protagonists.

SAGACIOUS adj. (SA-GAY-SHUS) wise, shrewd

Her grandfather, a *sagacious* old world publisher, suggested she attempt straight fiction first so as not to get too bogged down with research.

SALLOW adj. a sickly, greenish-yellow tone

Sasha didn't leave her room for weeks and as she struggled to create a storyline her complexion grew *sallow*.

SALLY n. a rushing attack, witty repartee, a brief excursion

Sasha watched out her window as a squirrel made a sudden *sally* across the street.

Sasha *sallied* (v.) across her room and downstairs to the front door, wondering if a bit of fresh air might not free her creative juices.

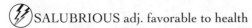

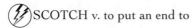 SALUBRIOUS adj. favorable to health

Sasha hoped the blue skies, green grass, and colorful flowers would have a *salubrious* effect on her physical and emotional health.

SANGFROID n. (SANG-FRWA) extraordinary composure in the face of danger

Just then a car came barreling down the street directly towards Sasha, who, exhibiting amazing *sangfroid*, quickly stepped up on the curb with merely a sigh.

SARTORIAL adj. relating to dress or fashion

Sasha used to take great pride in her *sartorial* flair, but lately had become downright dowdy in her dress.

SATURNINE adj. (SAT-ERR-NEYEN) sullen, gloomy, depressed

Everyone, most particularly her esteemed grandfather, noticed the *saturnine* turn Sasha's personality had taken lately .

SAVANT n. (SA-VON) a scholar, a very knowledgeable person

After giving the matter much thought he decided to put Sasha in touch with his most illustrious writer, a *savant* in the matters of artistic expression.

SCOFFLAW n. (SKAF-LAW) one who is continually breaking the law

Sasha's habit of befriending *scofflaws* served the purpose of keeping her life colorful and rife with storytelling possibility.

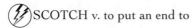 SCOTCH v. to put an end to

Her grandfather hoped to *scotch* these draining friendships with the help of his illustrious author.

SECRETE v. (SE-KRETE) to give off, to conceal

He did not realize this author *secreted* a foul odor.

The *secretion* (n.) was most offensive.

Whenever the grandfather had come to his home for a visit the author *secreted* his medicines behind locked doors to hide the fact of his illness.

SENTENTIOUS adj. preachy, pompous, using wise sayings excessively

Sasha's grandfather did not realize his literary savant could behave like a *sententious* jerk, and was informed of this only too late, by Sasha.

SHIBBOLETH n. a distinctive word or behavior that typifies a group, a slogan

"That you would think a gifted writer is a person worth knowing is a *shibboleth* of your profession," Sasha pronounced haughtily before she stomped off to begin the historical novel she felt finally ready to write.

 Plug In

Plug in your answers to see if you've made the right connections.
Match the word to its correct definition:

__	1. RUBRIC	(a)	healthful
__	2. RUMINATE	(b)	fashion
__	3. SAGACIOUS	(c)	scholar
__	4. SALLOW	(d)	sullen
__	5. SALLY	(e)	criminal
__	6. SALUBRIOUS	(f)	composure under fire
__	7. SANGFROID	(g)	slogan
__	8. SARTORIAL	(h)	put an end to
__	9. SATURNINE	(i)	wise
__	10. SAVANT	(j)	pompous
__	11. SCOFFLAW	(k)	category
__	12. SCOTCH	(l)	wander
__	13. SECRETE	(m)	to give off
__	14. SENTENTIOUS	(n)	to ponder
__	15. SHIBBOLETH	(o)	greenish skin tone

☼ *Recharge*

Here are the answers to this quiz. Check to see if you made the right connections! Test yourself again on the ones you missed.

1.	k	6.	a	11.	e
2.	n	7.	f	12.	h
3.	i	8.	b	13.	m
4.	o	9.	d	14.	j
5.	l	10.	c	15.	g

lesson 38

Is Sy a Stalwart Spelunker, or a Simpering Sycophant?

SIMPER v. to smile foolishly

> "Stop *simpering* and own up to your mistake," Sy, the electrician, told his apprentice.

SINE QUA NON n. (SIN-AY-KWA-NON) something that is an essential condition of

> "Making mistakes, is the *sine qua non* of being a novice," the apprentice shot back, clearly no fool.

SINUOUS adj. winding, having many curves

> "This wire, unfortunately follows a *sinuous* path through the wall," Sy observed.

> "The *sinuosity* (n.) of this wire might be responsible for the trouble it has been causing."

SLATTERNLY adj. squalid, a slovenly woman

> The *slatternly* homeowner suddenly walked by looking as unkempt and dirty as a homeless person.

> The electrician also observed the *slatternly* condition of the home with disgust.

SOMNOLENT adj. drowsy, sleepy

> As Sy droned on with instructions, the apprentice grew *somnolent* — he'd been out late the night before.

Somnolence (n.) threatened to overcome the apprentice who had begun the day with a hangover.

SPATE n. a sudden outburst

Suddenly, the homeowner reappeared and in a trembling voice cried out, "I just heard there's been a *spate* of robberies in the neighborhood! Are you two sure you're electricians and not robbers?"

SPELUNKER n. a cave explorer

"No," the weary apprentice responded dryly. "Actually we're *spelunkers*," he continued, pulling out his flashlight and shining it over the walls as if they were all standing in a cave.

STALWART adj. unwavering, robust, sturdily built

The woman turned *stalwart* in her insistence on seeing proper identification.

STRIATED adj. (STRY-AY-TED) marked with thin lines or grooves

"Why is your ID so *striated*?" she quizzed, flashing a suspicious look at the electrician and then staring back down at the oddly scratched plastic.

STURM AND DRANG n. turmoil

"During the *sturm and drang* of our last job, I accidentally dropped it under a kitchen appliance meant for slicing onions," Sy replied.

SUI GENERIS adj. (SOO-EE- GEN-ER-ISS) unique, of its own kind, in a class by itself

"Such a clever explanation can only mean you are *sui generis*," the woman said.

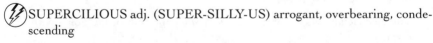SUPERCILIOUS adj. (SUPER-SILLY-US) arrogant, overbearing, condescending

"For a woman who comports herself like a filthy slob, you have some nerve coming on to us in such a *supercilious* manner," the drowsy apprentice commented with no regard for his position as freelance employee.

(⚡)SURREPTITIOUS adj. sneaky, secret

"You look perfectly capable of having a *surreptitious* motive to me."

"How do I know you haven't been *surreptitiously* (adv.) casing the joint?" the woman snapped, ignoring his insult.

(⚡)SYCOPHANT n. (SICK-O-FANT) a flatterer, a self-serving yes-man

"Oh, I can see how you would feel that way. You're obviously a very perceptive woman," Sy lept into the fray, desperate to keep the job but feeling a bit like a *sycophant*.

SYLLOGISM n. a form of logic in which major and minor premises are made and a conclusion drawn, a process of deduction

"All electricians are capable of disarming an alarm system," the woman mused. "You are an electrician. Therefore, you could disarm my alarm." She paused. "It's a simple *syllogism*, I know, but it's good enough for me. Get out." And she opened her front door.

Plug In

Plug in your answers to see if you've made the right connections.
Which of the sentences below use the words correctly?

1. Bette simpered with delight as she delivered a moving acceptance speech.
   CORRECT   INCORRECT

2. Tripping on a triple axel during competition is the sine qua non of learning the ins and outs of handling pressure.
   CORRECT   INCORRECT

3. Madeleine walked the sinuous path through the forest on her own as it was a simple, straight shot.
   CORRECT   INCORRECT

4. The slatternly woman walked into the employment center dressed impeccably and carrying a neat attache case.
   CORRECT   INCORRECT

5. After several hours of driving Neal experienced a fair degree of somnolence, as the highway seemed to stretch out before him endlessly.
   CORRECT   INCORRECT

6. There had been a spate of cheating episodes in the sixth-grade class, and so the principal called a special assembly to discuss the issues of honesty and hard work.

    CORRECT   INCORRECT

7. The spelunker, unaware that his tank was running out of oxygen, moved slowly through the water, admiring the array of magnificent fish.

    CORRECT   INCORRECT

8. The sailor was stalwart in his total insistence that he had not abandoned his post.

    CORRECT   INCORRECT

9. The road was striated with tire marks.

    CORRECT   INCORRECT

10. "Stop with the sturm and drang," Elizabeth snapped at her bickering employees.

    CORRECT   INCORRECT

11. The mail carrier, having delivered the mail everyday for a month without having to face a snow storm, considered herself sui generis.

    CORRECT   INCORRECT

12. "I am the best there is," Rashawnda announced in a supercilious tone.

    CORRECT   INCORRECT

13. Sylvia walked up to the guard surreptitiously and boldly asked, "Can you tell me where to find the Rembrandts?"

    CORRECT   INCORRECT

14. "I frankly don't care how you feel," Paul remarked, every inch the syco-phant.

    CORRECT   INCORRECT

15. Girls like boys. You are a boy. Therefore, you like girls. This is not a silly syllogism.

    CORRECT   INCORRECT

The answer key appears on the following page.

☀Recharge

Here are the answers to this quiz. Check to see if you made the right connections! In a few days, test yourself again on the ones you missed.

1.	incorrect	6.	correct	11.	incorrect
2.	correct	7.	incorrect	12.	correct
3.	incorrect	8.	correct	13.	incorrect
4.	incorrect	9.	correct	14.	incorrect
5.	correct	10.	correct	15.	correct

lesson 39

Is Tendentious Todd Temporizing?

SYLVAN adj. (SILL-VAN) forestlike, wooded

The scene projected on the conference room screen was of a lovely bench in a *sylvan* setting and underneath ran a poetic copy line.

SYNERGY n. the combined force of two distinct elements that is more powerful than each alone.

The *synergy* between Andy the copywriter, and Todd the graphic artist, was awesome.

Their *synergistic* (adj.) relationship garnered the attention of the advertising agent president.

The *synthesis* (n.) of their work produced a fabulous campaign.

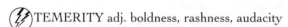TEMERITY adj. boldness, rashness, audacity

Part of what made Andy and Todd so exceptional as a team was their amazing *temerity*, which usually resulted in an attention-grabbing advertising concept.

TEMPORIZE v. to compromise, to draw something out in order to gain time

They refused to *temporize* their vision for the sake of others who were less confident in ground breaking approaches.

Andy would, however, *temporize* an explanation of his vision in order to give others the chance to come around to his way of thinking.

TENDENTIOUS adj. advancing a point of view, biased

Andy was accused by the creative director of being exceedingly *tendentious*, and not nearly open enough to the opinion of others.

TIMOROUS adj. fearful, easily frightened

Norita, Todd's and Andy's assistant, was a *timorous* sort, and was forever warning them to not be so aggressive in their stance at meetings.

TITULAR adj. in title only

"Don't worry," Andy would always say. "The *titular* head of the meeting is the director, Nathan, but I run the show."

TONY adj. fashionable, trendy, aristocratic,

"He is quite a *tony* fellow," Todd agreed, "but underneath his style and polish is an uncreative, uninspired brain."

TOOTHSOME adj. tasty, sexually attractive, luscious

As Todd spoke, Andy busied himself with adjusting his tie and striking a *toothsome* pose in the reflection of the window.

TRICE n. an moment, a short period of time

"I'm just afraid," said Norita, "that if you two were fired, I'd be gone in a *trice*."

⚡TRUCULENT adj. hostile, aggressive, savage

"The only person at this agency *truculent* enough to fire us is too busy annihilating the accounts-payable department to even notice us," Andy laughed.

UMBRAGE n. displeasure or resentment, shade

"I take *umbrage* at that remark," Norita snapped, "as you don't understand how dire my financial situation really is."

They were standing beneath the *umbrage* of a gazebo on the company grounds.

UNDULATE v. to move smoothly in a wavelike manner

All three turned to watch the *undulations* of the new receptionist, as she emerged from the building entrance, and walked to her car.

USURY n. (YOUZ-ERY) lending money at a high interest rate

"Would you think it *usury* if I ask to borrow a weeks' salary," Norita suddenly announced, "and pay you back with a home cooked meal every night?"

"I would think that would make me a very clever *usurer*!" Andy laughed.

⚡VACUOUS adj. empty, lacking intelligence

"*Vacuous* I'm not," said Norita, clearly proud of her ability to think with depth and respond with humor and flare.

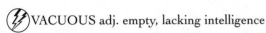 Plug In

Plug in your answers to see if you've made the right connections.
Choose the correct definition for each word.

1. SYLVAN
    a) green
    b) wooded
    c) silvery

2. SYNERGY
    a) power of two, combined
    b) alike
    c) boldness

3. TEMERITY
    a) rhythm
    b) fearfulness
    c) audacity

4. TEMPORIZE
    a) to calm
    b) to compromise
    c) to lecture

5. TENDENTIOUS
   a) biased
   b) hostile
   c) brutal

6. TIMOROUS
   a) well timed
   b) fearful
   c) angry

7. TITULAR
   a) royalty
   b) fashionable
   c) in title only

8. TONY
   a) aristocratic
   b) pompous
   c) snobby

9. TOOTHSOME
   a) long in the tooth
   b) attractive
   c) awkward

10. TRICE
    a) three times
    b) in a moment
    c) tricky

11. TRUCULENT
    a) large
    b) stubborn
    c) savage

12. UMBRAGE
    a) offense
    b) recklessness
    c) interest

13. UNDULATE
    a) move under
    b) to speed up
    c) to move wavelike

14. USURY
    a) high interest loan
    b) a manipulator
    c) someone in need

15. VACUOUS
    a) violent
    b) empty
    c) bold

⚡ Recharge

Here are the answers to this quiz. Check to see if you made the right connections! Test yourself again on the ones you missed.

1.	b	6.	b	11.	c
2.	a	7.	c	12.	a
3.	c	8.	a	13.	c
4.	b	9.	b	14.	a
5.	a	10.	b	15.	b

lesson 40

Is Zaftig Zillia Like a Zephyr?

VAGARY n. whim, an unpredictable action

> Due to the *vagaries* of the villagers it was unclear of they would band together to fight the dragon or if they would decide it was each man for himself.

VAINGLORIOUS adj. boastful, pompous

> The young butcher, Alphonso, purported to be the village's savior but it was a *vainglorious* claim.

VENEER n. facade, coating, outward appearance

> Alphonso wielded a golden sword with an oak *veneer* handle.

VENERATE v. to honor, to worship, to respect

> Alphonso was *venerated* by none, but was the object of amusement to many.

VERACIOUS adj. truthful, honest

> The village cobbler, a frightened but *veracious* man, admitted to his fear and then undertook to find a warrior brave enough to face the dragon.

VERDANT adj. covered with green plants, leafy

> He traveled into the *verdant* woods armed only with a map and sense of desperate urgency.

VICARIOUS adj. acting for another, sharing in an experience of another through the imagination

Stopping to watch two young men wrestle in a glade, the cobbler received *vicarious* pleasure imagining himself as the victor.

VISCOSITY adj. a thick or sticky consistency of a liquid

Suddenly the cobbler noticed his feet were planted in a liquid of such *viscosity* he couldn't move, and after studying the substance more closely realized it was dragon saliva.

VITRIOLIC adj. corrosive, biting, bitterly scathing

The two young men grew *vitriolic* as their match heated up, screaming all manner of insult at each other, and so neither noticed the cobbler's plight.

WASTREL n. someone who wastes, a spendthrift

One of them was clearly a *wastrel*, as he was bedecked in velvet and ermine, and yet it was obvious he was merely a peasant.

WIZENED adj. shriveled, withered

Just as the cobbler was about to call out, a *wizened* old woman appeared and exclaimed with great emotion, "Away! The dragon will be here anon!"

WONT n. custom, habit

"It is my *wont* to run from danger," the cobbler responded humbly, "but I am stuck in the dragon's excretions."

ZAFTIG adj. full-figured, plump

"I shall help you," cried out a sweet voice, and moments later a *zaftig* young peasant girl sprinted to the cobbler's side, threw him over her shoulder, and sped away, before either of the wrestlers could do a thing.

ZEITGEIST n. (ZITE-GISTE) the mood or spirit of the times

It was the *zeitgeist* of those days to find heroism in the most unlikely of places and within the hearts of the most unexpected people. This hero was named Zillia.

ZEPHYR n. (ZEF-ER) a gentle breeze

An hour later the dragon appeared but a sudden *zephyr* rustled the tree tops, and the beast, lulled by the gentle swishing noise, simply fell asleep, whereupon Alphonso appeared and not so bravely cut off his head.

Plug In
Using the words below, fill in the blanks.

(a) vagary	(f) verdant	(k) wizened
(b) vainglorious	(g) vicarious	(l) wont
(c) veneer	(h) viscosity	(m) zaftig
(d) venerated	(i) vitriolic	(n) zeitgeist
(e) veracious	(j) wastrel	(o) zephyr

1. Mai Yang took _____ pleasure in her daughter's accomplishments.

2. The liquid had such _____ the child mistook it for glue.

3. The forest is _____ in the summer.

4. The _____ cooled the valley.

5. The _____ old man lived by himself in the boarded up mansion.

6. Though a breakfast of asparagus and cheese was an odd choice, it was Maria's _____ to order it each morning.

7. It was the _____ of the century to be carefree and irresponsible.

8. The students _____ the dean for his years of devoted service to the university.

9. Rose Ellen had become a _____, spending money everywhere on completely unnecessary items.

10. Janet's _____ language hurt Diana terribly.

11. Vicki's_____ figure won her lots of attention from the opposite sex.

12. The general's _____ manner offended almost everyone he met for they knew he was really a coward.

13. Lisa, knowing the _____ of the weather, was reluctant to plan an outdoor wedding.

14. Mr. Torres was _____ in his consideration of all the facts, as he wished to reach a verdict based on truth.

15. The desk had a lovely _____ but was probably built poorly.

Recharge

Here are the answers to this quiz. Check to see if you made the right connections! Test yourself again on the ones you missed.

1. g	6. l	11. m
2. h	7. n	12. b
3. f	8. d	13. a
4. o	9. j	14. e
5. k	10. i	15. c

SECTION 3

Words to the Third Power: Really Hard Words You Ought to Know

Is Angie's Agathism the Opposite of Atheism?

ABLUTION n. the act of washing one's body

Angie finished her *ablutions* and then climbed, sadly, into bed.

ABNEGATE v. to deny to oneself, renounce, surrender

She had refused to *abnegate* her responsibility for the unfortunate accident that had befallen Jamie, her young charge.

ACIDULOUS adj. (ASID-YOU-LUS) sour, ill tempered

The child could be quite *acidulous*, and was partly responsible for cutting himself on the glass he had purposefully shattered.

ADVENTITIOUS adj. accidental

Angie had considered presenting the incident as *adventitious* but decided it was best to tell the truth.

AFFLATUS n. (AF-FLATE-IS) a creative impulse, divine inspiration

Lying in bed Angie experienced an *afflatus* so powerful she leaped from beneath the covers and flew to her sketch pad.

AGATHISM n. (A-GUH-THIZM) the belief that things ultimately lead to good

She was sure Jamie's accident would teach him to hold his temper and this *agathism* suddenly seemed to demand expression in an art form.

AGNATE n. from the father's side of the family

Angie had gotten her agathism from her *agnate* grandfather who spent his life looking at the bright side.

ALEATORY adj. (AY-LEE-A-TORY) based on chance

Her *aleatory* decision to tell Jamie's parents of his destructive temper would yield, she knew, possibly unpleasant results in the morning.

ANA n. a collection of materials that reflect a person or place

Angie, stopped her feverish drawing to consider her portfolio, an *ana* that seemed to trace the many phases of her life.

ANIMUS n. hostile feeling

She realized that is Jamie's parents had *animus* toward her, she'd use the opportunity to go back to art school.

Plug In

Match each word with its definition:

___	1. ABLUTION	(a)	accidental
___	2. ABNEGATE	(b)	creative inspiration
___	3. ACIDULOUS	(c)	collection of items
___	4. ADVENTITIOUS	(d)	based on chance
___	5. AFFLATUS	(e)	from the father's side
___	6. AGATHISM	(f)	hostile feeling
___	7. AGNATE	(g)	renounce
___	8. ALEATORY	(h)	belief that things lead to good
___	9. ANA	(i)	act of cleansing
___	10. ANIMUS	(j)	ill tempered

Recharge

Here are the answers to this quiz. Check to see if you made the right connections! Test yourself again on the ones you missed.

1.	i	6.	h
2.	g	7.	e
3.	j	8.	d
4.	a	9.	c
5.	b	10.	f

Is the Arriviste Bilious or Atrabilious?

ANTEDILUVIAN adj. extremely old, antiquated

"That wallpaper looks positively *antediluvian*," Lynnette commented as she walked into the musty old room.

ANTINOMY n. a contradiction between two seemingly true statements

"There is an *antinomy* surrounding that paper," Alyssa, the realtor, asserted. "One local historian is convinced it's of the early 19th century while another, the late 18th."

APHASIA n. loss of speech

Suddenly the realtor collapsed, and when she came to hours later was diagnosed with *aphasia*; she had suffered a stroke.

APHORISM n. a wise saying

The old town doctor who was given to *aphorisms* such as "still waters run deep" refrained from using them when comforting the family.

ARABLE adj. suitable for the growing of crops

The fields outside the realtor's home were quite *arable*, and so her family, worried about expenses, sold them off.

ARRANT adj. notoriously without moderation, downright

The realtor's father, Mick, an *arrant* manipulator, got everyone in town to contribute their particular expertise to the undertaking.

ARRIVISTE n. a social climber, an upstart

> In his younger years Mick had been known as an *arriviste*, but having failed to reach the heights he imagined for himself, he was now seen as slightly pathetic.

ASEPTIC adj. surgically clean, free of germs

> The realtor's family did their best to keep her environment *aseptic* so as to minimize the chance of infection.

ATRABILIOUS adj. inclined to melancholy

> Alyssa did her best to affect a cheery manner, but she had been *atrabilious* even before the stroke, and she could not even manage a smile.

BAILIWICK n. a particular area of expertis

> Marcia decided to re-wallpaper Alyssa's sick room for her; interior decorating was her *bailiwick*.

▓ Plug In

Plug in your answers to see if you've made the right connection.
Choose the correct definition:

1. ANTEDILUVIAN
    (a) opposed
    (b) antiquated
    (c) deluded

2. ANTINOMY
    (a) opposites
    (b) contradiction in ideas
    (c) contradiction between two seeming facts

3. APHASIA
    (a) loss of memory
    (b) loss of speech
    (c) loss of sanity

4. APHORISM
   (a) a witticism
   (b) a word play
   (c) a wise saying

5. ARABLE
   (a) easily likable
   (b) humorous
   (c) suitable for crops

6. ARRANT
   (a) total without moderation
   (b) always going against the grain
   (c) full of energy

7. ARRIVISTE
   (a) a newcomer
   (b) a social climber
   (c) an imposter

8. ASEPTIC
   (a) germ free
   (b) unusual
   (c) harsh

9. ATRABILIOUS
   (a) bad tempered
   (b) unkind
   (c) given to melancholy

10. BAILIWICK
    (a) belongings
    (b) area of expertise
    (c) special interest

·Ö·Recharge

Here are the answers to this Quiz. Check to see if you've made the right connections! Test yourself again on the ones you missed.

1. b	6. a
2. c	7. a
3. b	8. a
4. c	9. c
5. c	10. b

Does Bibulous Braggadocio Befit a Bellwether?

BANAUSIC adj. routine, mechanical, boring

Beth, distressed by weighty responsibilities, felt her life had become totally *banausic*.

BELLWETHER n. a person who assumes a leadership role or takes initiative

She envied her friend Shannon, a true *bellwether* in her chosen field, who led a life of exploration and excitement.

BENISON n. blessing, benediction

Shannon felt Beth's *benisons* were many, in particular when it came to her children, who were lovely and thriving.

BIBULOUS adj. highly absorbent, given to or fond of alcoholic beverages

Beth, in a very sour mood one evening, embarked on a *bibulous* journey, hopping from bar to bar.

BIFURCATED adj. forked, divided into two branches

Finally she realized she'd reached the proverbial *bifurcated* road, where she could either take that last possibly dangerous drink, or simply go home, tipsy but safe.

BOONDOGGLE n. a useless or valueless project or activity

Beth then decided in her bibulous state, that her business was nothing but a *boondoggle*.

BOSKY adj. wooded, covered with trees and shrubs

> She decided to take off on a road trip. The next morning, she rented a jeep, and an hour later stopped in a *bosky* area where she picked some wild flowers.

BRAGGADOCIO n. (BRAG-GA-DOE-SHE-O) arrogant pretension, empty conceit

> She then sat down and with great *braggadocio* wrote a few postcards describing her solo journey.

BRUMMAGEM adj. (BRUM-MA-JEM) bogus, fraudulent, cheap, showy

> Suddenly an elderly man wandered over, bedecked in *brummagem* jewels, and began to mutter, tremulously, an incantation.

CADUCITY n. (KA-DOO-CITY) the frailty of old age, the quality of being perishable, transitoriness

> Beth, quite perturbed, was reminded of her own impending *caducity*, and anxiously raced home.

Plug In

Plug in your answers to see if you've made the right connection.
Which of the following sentences are correct?

1. The Arctic explorer led a banausic life during every trek.
    CORRECT INCORRECT

2. Yalana was a bellwether when it came to committee work, always staying the background.
    CORRECT INCORRECT

3. She considered her work at the hospital full of benisons.
    CORRECT INCORRECT

4. Jack could tell the ride would be bibulous as it was dark and the roads were serpentine.
    CORRECT INCORRECT

5. The river was bifurcated near the huge oak tree and Tim couldn't decide which way to travel.

                         CORRECT   INCORRECT

6. Mr. Neruda went on a critical boondoggle to company headquarters in order to save the jobs of hundreds of employees.

                         CORRECT   INCORRECT

7. It was easy to run through the bosky terrain.

                         CORRECT   INCORRECT

8. Tim's braggadocio got him into a confrontation he'd have rather avoided.

                         CORRECT   INCORRECT

9. An assortment of brummagem antiques filled one aisle of the odd five and dime store.

                         CORRECT   INCORRECT

10. Aware of her caducity, the sick patient decided to draw up a will.

                         CORRECT   INCORRECT

⚡Recharge

Here are the answers to this Quiz. Check to see if you've made the right connections! Test yourself again on the ones you missed.

1. incorrect
2. incorrect
3. correct
4. incorrect
5. correct

6. incorrect
7. incorrect
8. correct
9. correct
10. correct

Did the Claque Clap at the Clique's Canard?

CANARD n. a fabricated story, or sensational report, a hoax

The ambitious reporter created the absurd *canard* that aliens were living in the mayor's basement, dining on mice.

CELERITY n. (SEL-ER-IT-EE) haste, swiftness of movement

He claimed the aliens, though not exactly runners, moved with great *celerity* as they skimmed here and there above the basement floor.

CENTRIFUGAL adj. proceeding in action away from the center or axle

An odd, scientific gauge of some kind, with an orbiting sensor that was spinning seemingly by *centrifugal* force, floated aimlessly just below the ceiling of the basement.

CLAQUE n. (KLAK) an audience paid to clap, an obsequious audience

The newspaper for which the reporter labored was worried the news conference would be a bust, and so they hired a *claque* to pretend enthusiasm for the reporter's exposé.

The wealthy and powerful editor-in-chief enjoyed a *claque* of followers who would do anything to gain his approval.

CLERISY n. the intellectual elite

The *clerisy* were deeply offended by the report and horrified that dignified newspapers were beginning to wonder if the possibility existed that Aliens might indeed be in the mayor's home.

CODICIL n. (COD-I-SILL) addition to a will

The reporter, having received many threats to his life, added a *codicil* to his will in order to make sure his young daughter would retain ownership of the Picasso hanging in his living room.

COEVAL adj. (KO-EE-VUL) originating during the same period

In his bedroom hung one oil painting that was *coeval* with another in the bathroom dating from the Italian Renaissance.

COMESTIBLES n. something that can be eaten as food

In his third piece the reporter described how the aliens considered all bugs and rodents *comestibles* and had virtually made the mayor's residence pest free.

CONCUPISCENCE n. ardent sexual desire

He also commented that the aliens seemed completely lacking in *concupiscence,* as they steered completely clear of each other, though he admitted he had no idea what sexual excitement between them might look like.

CONTRADISTINCTION n. in contrast with

The reporters perceptions were in direct *contradistinction* to those of the mayor, who exercised daily in his basement gym, and who claimed with no uncertainty, that there were neither aliens or mice on any of his machines.

▓ *Plug In*

Plug in your answers to see if you've the right connections.
Match each word with its correct definition.

__ 1. CANARD	(a) addition to a will
__ 2. CELERITY	(b) in contrast with
__ 3. CENTRIFUGAL	(c) a hoax
__ 4. CLAQUE	(d) a food stuff
__ 5. CLERISY	(e) sexual desire
__ 6. CODICIL	(f) action away from the center
__ 7. COEVAL	(g) intelligentsia
__ 8. COMESTIBLES	(h) a paid audience
__ 9. CONCUPISCENCE	(i) haste
__ 10. CONTRADISTINCTION	(j) from the same era

⚡Recharge

Here are the answers to this Quiz. Check to see if you've made the right connections! Test yourself again on the ones you missed.

1. c	6. a
2. i	7. j
3. f	8. d
4. h	9. e
5. g	10. b

Did David Desire a Demimonde or a Demitasse?

COMPENDIUM n. a comprehensive summary

David found a *compendium* of all the existing books on ornithology at the library.

CULVERT n. a sewer or drain

He didn't enjoy the research as the *culvert* under the street in front of the library was clearly malfunctioning and a stench was filling the austere building.

DAEDAL adj. (DEE-DULL) ingenious or complex in design

David had always loved the *daedal* design of the library floor plan which seemed mazelike to him and so he wandered about searching for fresh air.

DECIDUOUS adj. (DE-SID-YOO-OUS) shedding or losing leaves on a particular season, not evergreen

He particularly loved the *deciduous* plantings outside the library that so clearly marked seasonal changes.

DEFALCATE v. to embezzle

David, a retired executive who had just taken up bird watching, was saddened that his friend Stephan, who had been caught *defalcating*, was now in jail, unable to join him.

DEFENESTRATION n. the act of throwing someone or something out a window

His friend Stephan had considered the *defenestration* of evidence, but security entered his office just as he opened the window with the envelope in hand.

DEISM n. the belief that god created the world and then left it to its own devices.

David studied *deism*, believing that god created the world.

DEMIMONDE n. a class of kept women or women of lower social standing, a group that exists on the fringes of respectability

David finished his research and considered visiting the woman he kept, in the *demimonde*.

DENOUEMENT n. (DAY-NOO-MON) the outcome

David realized a public *denouement* of his associations in that world could be a rejection from his more erudite and respectable friends, but he didn't care.

DENUNCIATION n. (DE-NUN-SEE-A-SHUN) open condemnation

David would not countenance a single *denunciation* of his lifestyle.

Plug In

Plug in your answers to see if you've made the right connection.
Choose the correct definition for each word.

1. COMPENDIUM
   (a) collection
   (b) complete summary
   (c) design

2. CULVERT
   (a) secretive
   (b) crossing
   (c) drain

3. DAEDAL
    (a) complex
    (b) boring
    (c) low class

4. DECIDUOUS
    (a) fertile
    (b) determined
    (c) seasonally green

5. DEFALCATE
    (a) lie
    (b) embezzle
    (c) defy

6. DEFENESTRATION
    (a) making excuses
    (b) to defend angrily
    (c) the act of throwing something out a window

7. DEISM
    (a) the belief that God is all powerful
    (b) the belief that there are many gods
    (c) the belief that God made the world and then bowed out

8. DEMIMONDE
    (a) half the world
    (b) a fringe social group
    (c) criminals

9. DENOUEMENT
    (a) the climax
    (b) the build up
    (c) the outcome

10. DENUNCIATION
    (a) violence
    (b) sorrow
    (c) condemnation

🔅*Recharge*

Here are the answers to this Quiz. Check to see if you've made the right connections! Test yourself again on the ones you missed.

1.	b		6.	c	
2.	c		7.	c	
3.	a		8.	b	
4.	c		9.	c	
5.	b		10.	c	

Ellie Rules with Éclat and Eclairs!

DIADEM n. (DIE-A-DEM) a crown that indicates royalty,

Queen Ellie wore a sparkling *diadem* in her chocolate tresses.

DOLOROUS adj. (DO-LOR-US) sorrowful

Her *dolorous* cousin always walked ten paces behind her.

ÉCLAT n. (AY-KLOT) a dazzling success, acclaim

The Queen ruled her people with great *éclat*, winning their loyalty and inspiring them to self-sufficiency.

EDACIOUS adj. (EE-DAY-SHUS) having an insatiable appetite, great voracity

The only problem was that they had an *edacious* appetite for sweets, and the Queen was unable to attain enough Belgian chocolate to satisfy the ever-weakening masses.

EPHEMERAL adj. short-lived, transitory

She was able to secure some ersatz cocoa, but it had only an *ephemeral* taste and left the sweet-toothed even more desperate for the real thing.

EPICENE adj. (EH-PI-SEEN) having characteristics of both male and female, neuter

Finally the Queen made contact with the chocolate underground and was approached by an *epicene* figure with a voice that seemed neither male nor female.

ESCARPMENT n. cliff, a steep slope resulting from erosion

Exactly one week after her meeting with the epicene creature, the Queen once again met him/her on an *escarpment* near the sea, and was given a one-ton load of chocolate truffles and eclairs that almost toppled off the sharp slope.

ESCULENT adj. edible, suitable for eating

The Queen, unwilling to disappoint a single subject, bit off a piece to be sure it was more than simply *esculent*.

ETIOLATE adj. (EE-TEE-OH-LATE) pale and drawn, to make weak by stunting growth

She then hastened back to her kingdom to feed her subjects, for the lack of chocolate had rendered them *etiolated*.

EUTHENICS n. the science of improving the condition of humans by improving their environment

The Queen, a believer in *euthenics*, built a chocolate fence around the perimeter of her kingdom so that her subjects would feel sweetly embraced from all sides.

⟐ Plug In

Plug in your answers to see if you've made the right connections. Fill in the blanks with the correct words.

(a) diadem	(f) epicene
(b) dolorous	(g) escarpment
(c) éclat	(h) esculent
(d) edacious	(i) etiolated
(e) ephemeral	(j) euthenics

1. The _____ entourage followed the casket.

2. The sharp _____ suddenly appeared after the hurricane.

3. Janet was confused by the _____ appearance of her androgynous visitor.

4. The dish was prepared lovingly and was deemed excitingly _____.

5. The little boy seemed terribly _____ after his ordeal.

6. Dr. Rodriquez, believing in _____, recommended a month's respite in the country.

7. Wanda had an _____ appetite for shrimp whether they were fried, broiled, or smoked.

8) Jody had an _____ quality, making it difficult for anyone to get a grip on who she really was.

9. Eavan delivered the speech with tremendous _____, bringing everyone to his feet.

10. The _____ was placed on his head amidst much pomp.

⚙ *Recharge*

Here are the answers to this Quiz. Check to see if you've made the right connections! Test yourself again on the ones you missed.

1.	b		6.	j
2.	g		7.	d
3.	f		8.	e
4.	h		9.	c
5.	i		10.	a

Is Gregory a Galoot or a Grig?

EVANESCENT adj. (EE-VAN-ESS-ENT) fleeting, vanishing, transient

It seemed that everything the magician touched took on an *evanescent* quality.

EVINCE v. to show, reveal

Gregory, the magician, *evinced* a skill few could ignore.

FILIAL adj. (FILL-EE-UHL) relating to a son

He had a strong *filial* relationship with his esteemed teacher who died many years ago.

FROWARD adj. contrary, consistently disobedient

The older magician had taken in the young and *froward* Gregory, even though he was a callow youth given to revealing the tricks of the trade to anyone.

FUSTIAN adj. ridiculously pompous, bombastic, grandiose in delivery

Gregory would stand on street corners and in a *fustian* manner announce his intended magic trick.

GALOOT n. a loutish oaf, a clumsy but somewhat likable person

Most passersby thought he seemed a *galoot*, but they often stopped anyway to savor whatever wizardry he might evince.

GEMEINSCHAFT n. (GE-MEYEN-SHAFT) a group with similar tastes, a group bound by similar interests and kinship

The *gemeinschaft* of magicians with which the older magician associated, were not at first fond of Gregory, as they found him to be a lout.

GRIG n. a lively person

But as Gregory gained skill and thus, confidence, others began to view him more as a delightful *grig* than an annoying jerk.

HEGIRA n. (HEH-JEER-A) an escape to avoid danger or to get away from an unpleasant location

Gregory decided he would add storytelling to his act, and thus created monologues to introduce each trick which often included tales of an *hegira* undertaken across several continents by many a magician in order to protect the secrets of his magic.

HOMOLOGATE v. to confirm officially

Finally he was informed he had been admitted into the magician's union, though he did not believe it until it was *homologated* by his teacher and father.

Plug In

Plug in your answers to see if you've the right connections.
Match each word with its correct definition.

___	1. EVANESCENT	(a)	clumsy oaf
___	2. EVINCE	(b)	officially confirm
___	3. FILIAL	(c)	journey to escape danger
___	4. FROWARD	(d)	a lively person
___	5. FUSTIAN	(e)	a group united by kinship and interests
___	6. GEMEINSCHAFT	(f)	habitually contrary
___	7. GALOOT	(g)	to reveal
___	8. GRIG	(h)	fleeting
___	9. HEGIRA	(i)	pompous
___	10. HOMOLOGATE	(j)	related to a son

The answer key appears on the following page.

💡 *Recharge*

Here are the answers to this quiz. Check to see if you made the right connections! Test yourself again on the ones you missed.

1.	h		6.	e
2.	g		7.	a
3.	j		8.	d
4.	f		9.	c
5.	i		10.	b

Evan, Inured to the Ineluctable and Ineffable!

HORTATIVE adj. giving advice or exhortation

> The baseball coach gave a long and *hortative* talk to his young team, which unfortunately put them to sleep.

HUGGER-MUGGER n. a confusion, jumble, muddle

> Just before the game began there was a general *hugger-mugger* over the batting lineup.

IMAGO n. an adult stage of an insect, an ideal image of a parent formed in childhood and remaining unconscious in adulthood

> Evan, the coach's adult son, watched his father with the team and smiled, happily embracing the *imago* he still carried within.

INDETERMINATE adj. vague, not known in advance

> The game would go on for an *indeterminate* amount of time, and so the coach's son went out for a cup of coffee.

> He believed completely in *indeterminism* (n.), which was took the philosophical stand that everything in unpredictable.

INDUBITABLE adj. unquestionable

> That the coach was fully committed to the success of his team was an *indubitable* fact.

INEFFABLE adj. unutterable, unspeakable

Truthfully Evan found the games to be an *ineffable* bore, and so he admired his father all the more for his indefatigable interest.

INELUCTABLE adj. inescapable, not to be avoided

He had in truth never liked to play ball himself, but it had been in his childhood an *ineluctable* activity; he had surrendered to his father's wishes.

INQUIETUDE n. uneasiness, restlessness

There was an atmosphere of *inquietude* at home whenever he did resist playing, and so he had found it was best to go with the program.

INURED v. to become accustomed to something undesirable

Evan had become *inured* to his father's criticisms of his skills, convincing himself that he deserved the harsh words.

JEJUNE adj. dull, lacking interest, empty of food

Now, as a young man, Evan experienced great *jejune* when contemplating his youth, probably as a defense against his anger and resentment.

Plug In

Plug in your answers to see if you've made the right connections.
Choose the correct definition for each word.

1. HORTATIVE
   (a) giving advice
   (b) angrily
   (c) entreatingly

2. HUGGER-MUGGER
   (a) jumble
   (b) stupidity
   (c) hostility

3. IMAGO
   (a) a picture
   (b) a childhood ideal image
   (c) an illusion

4. INDETERMINATE
   (a) vague
   (b) unsure
   (c) lacking determination

5. INDUBITABLE
   (a) doubtful
   (b) unquestionable
   (c) depressing

6. INEFFABLE
   (a) unspeakable
   (b) impossible
   (c) ineffectual

7. INELECUTABLE
   (a) cannot be elected
   (b) cannot be done
   (c) cannot be escaped

8. INQUIETUDE
   (a) restlessness
   (b) noisiness
   (c) misery

9. INURED
   (a) angered
   (b) hardened
   (c) interested

10. JEJUNE
    (a) warm
    (b) bored
    (c) happy

☼ Recharge

Here are the answers to this quiz. Check to see if you made the right connections! Test yourself again on the ones you missed.

1.	a		6.	a
2.	a		7.	c
3.	b		8.	a
4.	a		9.	b
5.	b		10.	b

Lachrymose Logan Loved Leanna

LABILE adj. unstable, adaptable, liable to change

Little Logan was somewhat *labile* in mood, swinging in any given day from happy to sad several times over.

LACHRYMOSE adj. (LAK-RI-MOSE) tearful, mournful

He would grow particularly *lachrymose* when it was time for a friend to leave, often crying bitterly up to an hour after the actual departure.

LAMBENT adj. radiant, flickering, marked by lightness

Yet there was a *lambent* quality to Logan's smile that could put everyone around him into a glorious state of mind.

LISSOME adj. (LYE-SUM) supple

Leanna, his *lissome* nanny and aspiring actor, had taken up yoga to stay in shape.

LUMINARY n. a person of great intellectual, creative or spiritual stature

Logan's father was a *luminary* in the New York theater scene and traveled widely.

LUPINE adj. (LOO-PINE) having the characteristics of a wolf.

He had exotic amber eyes and arched eyebrows, and it was often commented that he had a rather *lupine* look about him, minus the bicuspids.

MANQUÉ adj. (MON-KAY) a failure to realize one's aspirations

Leanna had wanted to become a famous actor but had concluded early on that she was doomed to be an artist *manqué*.

MANUMIT v. to release from slavery

"Slaves everywhere yearn to be *manumitted* by their oppressive and cruel owners," Leanna burst forth to Logan's father, clutching her hands to her chest in an effort to increase the dramatic effect.

MATRIX n. something from which something else originates or takes form

Logan's father said gently, "New Yorkers think New York is the *matrix* of American culture. You live in New York, you have no excuse!"

MELANGE n. (MAY-LANGE) a mixture of incongruous elements

"My education has been a *melange* of varying dramatic techniques with an emphasis on none!" Leanna cried out with frustration.

Plug In

Plug in your answers to see if you've made the right connections Which of these sentences use the word correctly?

1. Dirk's medical condition was labile and thus quite difficult to manage.
    CORRECT   INCORRECT

2. Jose's lachrymose spirits helped everyone brighten right up.
    CORRECT   INCORRECT

3. The room had a lambent glow, perfect for a romantic evening.
    CORRECT   INCORRECT

4. The lissome woman worked out at the gym.
    CORRECT   INCORRECT

5. Jancha's lover was a luminary of such infamy that most ran when he entered a room.
    CORRECT   INCORRECT

6. His lupine looks and reputation drove his women made with desire.
    CORRECT   INCORRECT

7. Camille, the intellectual manqué, had written a much admired tome on European societies.

    CORRECT   INCORRECT

8. Lincoln hoped to manumit the slaves well before he was able to.

    CORRECT   INCORRECT

9. If you want to know what's wrong, look around at the matrix of the facility for clues.

    CORRECT   INCORRECT

10. There was a pitiful melange of materials in the art class which made it impossible for all the students to express themselves.

    CORRECT   INCORRECT

⋰○⋱ *Recharge*

Here are the answers to this quiz. Check to see if you made the right connections! Test yourself again on the ones you missed.

1.	correct	6.	correct
2.	incorrect	7.	incorrect
3.	correct	8.	correct
4.	correct	9.	incorrect
5.	incorrect	10.	incorrect

Did Marty's Minions Mouth a Moue or a Moo?

MIEN n. (MEEN) demeanor, the air or bearing of a person

Marty's *mien* was of someone under complete control.

MINION n. (MIN-YON) a hanger-on, a follower, an underling

He was surrounded by *minions* who lived for his every instruction.

MOUE n. (MOO) a pout, usually playful, a little grimace

Occasionally Marty would give vent to a *moue* in response to someone's stupid question.

MUGWUMP n. a person or politician who can't make up his mind, an independent

Marty was definitive in all decisions, but his boss was a miserable *mugwump*, and it drove Marty nuts.

NEFANDOUS adj. unspeakable, unutterable

In truth, Marty suspected his boss of being a *nefandous* embezzler, but he couldn't be sure.

NIMBUS n. an atmosphere that surrounds a person or thing, a rain cloud, a radiant light suggesting holiness

Marty noticed his boss walked around in a *nimbus* of angry unrest and expensive cologne.

OBLOQUY n (AH-BLA-KWEE) strong language of condemnation

He would have subjected his boss to his inner voice of *obloquy* but he preferred to secure himself another position.

OBSTREPEROUS adj. stubbornly defiant, angry and clamorous

The employees who worked directly under Marty's boss were becoming *obstreperous* in their demands for higher wages and more respect.

ODIUM n. (O-DEE-UM) the burden of the distastefulness of a particular act

Settling the conflict was an *odious* task.

OFFAL n. (OF-FUL) the waste parts of a product (often as in a butchered animal), refuse, rubbish

Finally, Marty's boss was demoted and put in charge of the company's *offal*, which in this case had something to do with animal innards.

Plug In
Plug in your answers to see if you've the right connection.
Match each word with its correct definition.

__	1. MIEN	(a)	public condemnation
__	2. MINION	(b)	evil
__	3. MOUE	(c)	demeanor
__	4. MUGWUMP	(d)	angrily stubborn
__	5. NEFANDOUS	(e)	atmosphere
__	6. NIMBUS	(f)	waster product
__	7. OBLOQUY	(g)	an indecisive person
__	8. OBSTREPEROUS	(h)	deserved loathing
__	9. ODIUM	(i)	a pout
__	10. OFFAL	(j)	a follower

The answer key appears on the following page.

☼ *Recharge*

Here are the answers to this quiz. Check to see if you made the right connections! Test yourself again on the ones you missed.

1. c	6. e
2. j	7. a
3. i	8. d
4. g	9. h
5. b	10. f

Is Pappas a Parvenu?

OPINE v. (OH-PINE) to express an opinion

Tia Pappas had been given the onerous task of finding Dr. Isabella Cordova in the heart of the jungle and secretly *opined* that it was fruitless.

PACE n. (PAY-SEE) with deference to

"I fervently expect, *pace* those who have gone before me, that I will find the good doctor, as I am traveling well equipped for the mission," she announced publicly nonetheless.

PACHYDERM n. (PACK-UH-DERM) a thick-skinned animal

"I also hope to photograph the *pachyderm* I encounter as I have been an avid fan of elephants all my life," Tia Pappas added, smiling gamely for the press.

PALIMPSEST n. a surface that has been written on, erased or covered, and then reused for something else

"I also hope to find, perhaps in yet undiscovered caves, fascinating *palimpsests* that will offer clues not just to the near past but also, underneath, to that of ancient times."

PARALOGISM n. illogical reasoning of which the reasoner is not aware

"Dr. Isabella Cordova, of course, has made an art form of *paralogism*, for though she intended to explore rain forests, her conclusion that going to any forest and waiting for it to rain, makes it difficult to pinpoint her possible location."

PAROXYSM n. (PAR-EX-IZM) a fit

"Of course I did try to explain this to her before she left," Tia Pappas continued, "but any attempt to straighten out her illogical thinking would send her into such *paroxysms* of violence it simply wasn't worth she effort."

PARVENU n. an upstart who has acquired wealth and class but hasn't achieved the social acceptance or position

"I believe that my partner in the venture, Ralph Guineas, a man of extraordinary bravery, will be a great help," Tia Pappas asserted, though truthfully she considered the newly wealthy man a *parvenu* and giant annoyance.

PASTICHE n. (PAS-TEESH) a piece that imitates or is made up from pieces of other works, a hodgepodge from different sources

"Our game plan for finding the good doctor will be a *pastiche* of approaches recommended by those who have traversed the difficult terrain before us."

PERCIPIENCE n. keen perception

A reporter of keen *percipience* suddenly asked, "What will you do if the mission is unsuccessful, as you are clearly a woman not used to failure?"

PERDITION n. eternal damnation

"I will consider that I have brought *perdition* upon myself, and rather than return I may devote the rest of my life to missionary work," Tia Pappas replied, bending down to wipe a smudge off her shiny black shoe.

🔌 *Plug In*

Plug in your answers to see if you've made the right connections.
Choose the correct definition.

1. OPINE
   (a) expressed
   (b) cried
   (c) demanded

2. PACE
   (a) heedless
   (b) involved
   (c) in deference to

3. PACHYDERM
   (a) a green plant
   (b) a thick-skinned animal
   (c) a snake

4. PALIMPSEST
   (a) rock formation
   (b) layered writing surface
   (c) bad weather

5. PARALOGISM
   (a) parallel thinking
   (b) military
   (c) illogical reasoning

6. PAROXYSM
   (a) confusion
   (b) depression
   (c) a fit

7. PARVENU
   (a) a traveler
   (b) a fake
   (c) wealthy person without stature

8. PASTICHE
   (a) hodgepodge
   (b) joke
   (c) ancient writing

9. PERCIPIENCE
   (a) doggedness
   (b) concept
   (c) perception

10. PERDITION
    (a) confusion
    (b) damnation
    (c) journey

☼·Recharge

Here are the answers to this quiz. Check to see if you made the right connections! Test yourself again on the ones you missed.

1.	a	6.	c
2.	c	7.	c
3.	b	8.	a
4.	b	9.	c
5.	c	10.	b

Phillipe, the Proselytizing Poltroon

PLENARY adj. complete, fully attended, not deficient in any way

Gil, the detective, had assembled a *plenary* dossier on Monique.

PLUVIAL adj. (PLOO-VEE-UL) rainy

It had been a *pluvial* day when he'd finally completed his investigations and he'd celebrated by stepping out of the rain into his favorite bar.

POLTROON n. a coward

The detective had gotten much of his information on Monique from her Phillipe, her ex, a true *poltroon*, who was so alarmed at the gumshoe's visit he couldn't stop talking.

PROSCENIUM n. the part of the stage in front of the curtain, the wall frame for the stage

He'd stood under the arched *proscenium*, shaped like the entrance to a mosque, and trembled pathetically as he'd chattered away.

PROSELYTIZE v. (PROS-E-LE-TIZE) to seek to convert someone to a religion, cause or political position

After coughing up everything he knew, Phillipe, a devout Catholic, *proselytized* so feverishly that Gil thought himself to be having a vision.

PULCHRITUDE v. (PULL-KRI-TUDE) physical beauty

Moments later he realized his "vision" was Simone, the show's leading lady dressed up as a Greek goddess.

QUA in the capacity of

The detective, *qua* lover, instantly followed her down stage to ask for her phone number.

QUIDDITY n. the real nature of a thing, the essence, a hairsplitting distinction

He was not in a hurry to get back to his office because the *quiddity* of Monique's life, as it turned out, was her devotion to her children.

The detective pondered the *quiddity* of her daily life and determined she was essentially a good-hearted citizen.

QUISLING n. a traitor who helps an enemy who occupies his country

Monique had been suspected of being a *quisling* during the war but the detective was quite sure she had not betrayed her country.

QUOTIDIAN adj. (KWO-TID-EE-EN) occurring every day, commonplace

The detective's request was a *quotidian* one for Simone, and she promptly gave him her agent's number, as she disliked refusing anyone anything. The detective never suspected.

Plug In

Plug in your answers to see if you've made the right connections.
Fill in the blanks with the correct words.

(a) plenary   (f) pulchritude
(b) pluvial   (g) qua
(c) poltroon   (h) quiddity
(d) proscenium   (i) quisling
(e) proselytize   (j) quotidian

1. Gilda attempted to _____, but no one would listen to her idealized version of the cult's lifestyle.

2. There was a _____ session of the PTA because of the impending budget cuts.

3. President Ginsberg, _____ father, attempted to take his daughter to the school play with as little fanfare as possible.

4. Her remarks seem humorous and joyful but their true _____ was lost on no one who listened carefully to the underlying message.

5. Rolf was accused of being a _____ when it was discovered he gave away the hiding place of his neighbors to the enemy.

6. Audre knew herself to be a complete _____ when it came to trying any sport that might be physically risky.

7. The criminal viewed each robbery as a _____ act, though he knew his victims were always surprised.

8. Chance, the set designer, stood back and admired the _____ which now framed the stage.

9. Adrienne possessed such _____ that no man could take his eyes off of her.

10. It had been a _____ day but somehow everyone's spirits had remained undampened.

Recharge

Here are the answers to this quiz. Check to see if you made the right connections! Test yourself again on the ones you missed.

1.	e		6.	c
2.	a		7.	j
3.	g		8.	d
4.	h		9.	f
5.	i		10.	b

Were the Satraps Sequacious or Loquacious?

RETINUE n. (RET-IN-OO) a group of attendants to an elevated person

The Emperor and his *retinue* swept past the crowds to bow before the memorial.

ROUÉ n. (ROO-AY) a lecherous man, a rake, a person devoted to sensual pleasures

The town *roué* thought it best not to appear—he had been having a secret affair with the Empress.

SAPOROUS adj. tasty, flavorsome

Besides, the roué had been invited to a *saporous* feast prepared by a former lover who was now the Emperor's chef.

SATRAP n. a subordinate ruler

The Emperor nodded at the numerous *satraps* who lined his path to the memorial, knowing they envied his lofty position.

SCIOLISM n. (SIGH-O-LIZM) superficial knowledge

The roué, anxious to appear not just sensual but also learned, displayed a *sciolism* that nevertheless impressed the illiterate chef.

SENESCENCE n. beginning of old age

He was forever having nightmares about *senescence* and so when not eating, the roué spent endless hours exercising and moisturizing his skin.

SEQUACIOUS adj. slavish, obsequious, following in logical sequence

The emperor enjoyed the ardor of the *sequacious* masses.

SERRIED adj. crowded together

During the memorial ceremony the citizens were *serried* in one of the palace's tiny courtyards.

SERVIETTE n. a table napkin

At about this time the roué was placing a lacy *serviette* upon his lap.

SHANTUNG n. a heavy nubby fabric, made of wild silk

Just then the Empress, draped in fuschia *shantung*, swept into the kitchen and begged the roué to depart—she was quite sure the Emperor would ultimately discover the identity of her lover.

Plug In

Plug in your answers to see if you've the right connections.
Match each word with its correct definition.

___ 1. RETINUE	(a)	crowded together
___ 2. ROUÉ	(b)	napkin
___ 3. SAPOROUS	(c)	subordinate leader
___ 4. SATRAP	(d)	rake
___ 5. SCIOLISM	(e)	nubby silk material
___ 6. SENESCENCE	(f)	onset of old age
___ 7. SEQUACIOUS	(g)	slavish
___ 8. SERRIED	(h)	superficial knowledge
___ 9. SERVIETTE	(i)	tasty
___ 10. SHANTUNG	(j)	followers

The answer key appears on the following page.

⌖Recharge

Here are the answers to this quiz. Check to see if you made the right connections! Test yourself again on the ones you missed.

1.	j		6.	f
2.	d		7.	g
3.	i		8.	a
4.	c		9.	b
5.	h		10.	e

lesson 54

Thomas—Not a Temararious Tatterdemalion

SUPERVENE v. to follow immediately after, to ensue

When the economy plummeted, a depression *supervened* in the town.

SURCEASE n. (SIR-SEESE) cessation

There was a spate of robberies and so the desperate mayor called for a *surcease* by filling the jails.

TATTERDEMALION n. a ragged person, always in tatters

Tatterdemalions everywhere foraged through the garbage for some food.

TELEOLOGY n. the study of design or purpose in natural phenomena

One tatterdemalion had been a *teleologist*, and had spent hours trying to understand the purpose of twin tornadoes, but now he was too hungry to much care.

TEMERARIOUS adj. recklessly daring, rash

One thief, upon breaking out of jail, undertook the *temerarious* heist of the decade, by breaking into C. P. Winston's and making off with the Indigo Diamond.

TENEBROUS adj. dark and gloomy

He was promptly caught and tossed in a *tenebrous* cell in the basement of the local jail.

TERMAGANT n. a quarrelsome woman, a shrew

To make matters worse his cell was next to that of a *termagant* who would not stop complaining and shrieking day and night.

TOR n. a high rock, a high rocky hill, or pile of rocks

High atop a *tor*, Thomas Bianchini, the wealthiest man in the area, looked down upon the impoverished town and wondered how they would manage.

TRILEMMA n. a problem for which there are three possible courses of action, and none perfect

He saw the situation as a *trilemma*, for if they continued stealing from each other, anarchy would reign. If they tried to manage with what each person had, someone would starve. And if they decided to seek their fortunes elsewhere, there was no guarantee anyone would survive the trek.

TUMID adj. (TOO-MID) swollen, distended, a bulging shape, overblown, bombastic

The wealthy man decided to give a speech outlining the possibilities but it was so *tumid* in style that no one listened and someone picked his pocket.

The pickpocket received a smack on the head that resulted in a *tumid* bruise just above his left eye.

Plug In

Plug in your answers to see if you've made the right connections. Choose the correct definition for each word.

1. SUPERVENE
   (a) to ensue
   (b) to succeed
   (c) to pass

2. SURCEASE
   (a) to seize
   (b) to surpass
   (c) cessation

3. TATTERDEMALION
   (a) flower
   (b) ragged criminal
   (c) ragged person

4. TELEOLOGY
   (a) study of mechanics
   (b) study of purpose behind natural phenomenon
   (c) study of paganism

5. TEMERARIOUS
   (a) rash
   (b) rude
   (c) wicked

6. TENEBROUS
   (a) gloomy
   (b) tense
   (c) loud

7. TERMAGANT
   (a) bad-tempered landlord
   (b) a shrew
   (c) a spoiled child

8. TOR
   (a) a high rocky hill
   (b) a large bird
   (c) a small village

9. TRILEMMA
   (a) a three-act play
   (b) a situation with three solutions, none great
   (c) a three-part job

10. TUMID
    (a) swollen
    (b) uncomfortable
    (c) dark

Recharge

Here are the answers to this quiz. Check to see if you made the right connections! Test yourself again on the ones you missed.

1. a
2. c
3. c
4. b
5. a

6. a
7. b
8. a
9. b
10. a

Did Willow Welter, Wither, or Winnow?

UKASE n. (YOU-KAZE) an authoritative decree, official edict

Willow Walker, the ambassador, suddenly issued an *ukase* that all snakes were to be considered holy.

USUFRUCT n. (YOO-ZOO-FRUCT) the right to use someone else's property as long as it's not damaged in the process

A few years earlier, Willow, employing *usufruct,* was on her way to her friend's empty country home.

VERNAL adj. occurring in spring, springlike youthful

It was a *vernal* evening and while she had felt driven to protect the snakes, she felt an equal pull by her fear of them.

VITIATE v. (VISH-EE-ATE) to impair the quality of, to corrupt morally

Long ago Willow had been *vitiated* by her mentor, Richard, who had used her innocence for personal gain.

VITUPERATIVE adj. harshly scolding, acrimonious

Willow upon discovering the true nature of their relationship had become quite *vituperative.*

VOTARY n. a person bound by vows to live a life of religious service

She visited a *votary* at her local parish but could find little solace.

WELTER v. to writhe, toss, wallow

She *weltered* about for a while, utterly confused as to whether or not to seek a reconciliation with her mentor, but finally decided against it.

WINNOW v. to blow of, or away, to separate the good from the bad

Willow imagined old folks *winnowing* wheat, separating the wheat from the chaff. She decided to live her life on her own terms.

WRAITH n. a specter, ghost of a dead person

Days later, the *wraith* of her dead mother appeared, insisting she protect all reptiles.

ZIGGURAT n. (ZIG-ER-AHT) a terraced temple tower constructed by the ancient Assyrians

After visiting her friend's home and walking through snake country, Willow made a pilgrimage to a *ziggurat* where she prayed for the strength to forgive her mentor and the wisdom to appreciate reptilian life. And that is how snakes came to be holy in that land.

Plug In

Plug in your answers to see if you've the right connections.
Match each word with its correct definition:

___ 1. UKASE	(a)	specter
___ 2. USUFRUCT	(b)	corrupt
___ 3. VERNAL	(c)	separate
___ 4. VITIATE	(d)	worshipper
___ 5. VITUPERATIVE	(e)	the right to use without harming something
___ 6. VOTARY	(f)	official edict
___ 7. WELTER	(g)	wallow
___ 8. WINNOW	(h)	a terraced temple
___ 9. WRAITH	(i)	harsh
___ 10. ZIGGURAT	(j)	springlike

The answer key appears on the following page.

Recharge

Here are the answers to this quiz. Check to see if you made the right connections! Test yourself again on the ones you missed.

1.	f	6.	d
2.	e	7.	g
3.	j	8.	c
4.	b	9.	a
5.	i	10.	h

Root Juice

Knowing the roots of words can help us figure out new words we don't know. Root juice can boost our vocabulary power. *Etymology* refers to the study of roots, and how words can grow!

Here's an example of a root growing words:

> The roots SED/SESS/SID mean to sit, to be still, to plan, to plot. Now, consider the words preSIDe, disSIDent, inSIDious, obSESSion.

That's the good news. It's no small potatoes. Here's another one.

> Look at FIN (end). Consider deFINitive, FINale, conFINe.
Great, huh?!

But don't get too excited. Roots offer the common heritage of words thousands of years old. But things have changed a lot. Roots don't always point the way.

> Example: *affinity* is also of the root, FIN. But *affinity* means a kinship, or attractive force.

Of course sometimes the meaning is close, but the spelling has kind of gone haywire.

> Example: *cogent*, is actually of the root, ACT/AG (to do, to drive to lead) *Cogent* means convincing, having the power to compel. That's somewhat close in meaning, but you can see what we mean about the spelling.

There are other problems with using roots to pinpoint a definition. The etymology of a word is a great trick if you know Greek, or Latin, or French. For example, DEM in Greek means "people." *DEMocracy* essentially means government of the people. Neat and tidy. Right? Sure, but look what you've got to get right first. It helps if you study and learn where there are exceptions.

Example: The word *venal.* The root VEN/VENT means to come, to move toward. But *venal* means corrupt or capable of being bought. *Adventure, convene, event, avenue, advent,* and *circumvent* clearly spring from the root meaning. *Venal* is a bit of a stretch.

Another Example: The word *pediatrician* has PED for a root. PED has to do with the foot. But a *pediatrician* is a children's doctor. A *podiatrist* is a foot doctor.

As it turns out the etymology of a word is merely a good trick. It can help you figure out and remember the meaning of a word. But it won't every time and certainly can't provide the basic definition of a word. It may even mess you up.

So why bother? Because if you don't have a clue what a word means, you have to start somewhere. Roots are an efFICacious place to begin. (FIC: to do, to make.) And this is not an OBfuscation. You figure it out.

Common Roots

The common roots are explained here, in alphabetical order. For each root, we've provided definitions, of some words containing the root. For the last word in each list, we used the word in a sample sentence. See if you can figure out the meaning of the word based on its root.

A: Without
>*amoral:* not moral, not immoral
>*atheist:* one who does not believe in God
>*atypical:* not typical
>*anonymous:* something of unknown origin
>*apathy:* without interest or emotion
>*atrophy:* the wasting away of body tissue
>*anomaly:* an irregularity
>*agnostic:* one who questions the existence of God
>
>The glob of paint resting on the canvas was rather *amorphous.*

AB/ABS: off, away from, apart, down (Latin)
>*abduct:* to take by force
>*abhor:* to hate, detest
>*abolish:* to do away with, make void
>*abstract:* conceived apart from concrete realities, specific objects, or actual instances
>*abnormal:* deviating from a standard
>*abdicate:* to renounce or relinquish a throne

abstinence: forbearance from any indulgence of appetite
abstruse: hard to understand; secret, hidden

The behavior of Maurice, the painter, was so *aberrant* that the dealer felt compelled not to show his work.

AC/ACR: sharp, bitter (Latin)

acid: something that is sharp, sour, or ill natured
acute: sharp at the end; ending in a point
acerbic: sour or astringent in taste; harsh in temper
exacerbate: to increase bitterness or violence; aggravate
acrid: sharp or biting to the taste or smell
acrimonious: caustic, stinging, or bitter in nature

Maurice, however, had a great deal of financial *acumen* and convinced the dealer to accept his peculiarities.

ACT/AG: to do, to drive, to force, to lead (Latin)

agile: quick and well coordinated in movement; active, lively
agitate: to move or force into violent, irregular action
exacting: unduly severe in demands and requirements
litigate: to make the subject of a lawsuit
prodigal: wastefully or recklessly extravagant
pedagogue: a teacher
synagogue: a gathering or congregation of Jews for the purpose of religious worship.

The dealer hoped his *exacting* standards would not be compromised by his decision to work with Maurice.

AD/AL: to, toward, near (Latin)

adapt: adjust or modify fittingly
adjacent: lying near, close, or contiguous; adjoining
addict: to give oneself over, as to a habit or pursuit
admire: to regard with wonder, pleasure, and approval
address: to direct a speech or written statement to
adhere: to stick fast; cleave; cling
adjoin: to be close or in contact with
advocate: to plead in favor of

The dealer, after watching Maurice work a room, had to admit that Maurice had no small amount of personal *allure*.

AL/ALI/ALTER: other, another (Latin)

alternative: a possible choice

alias: an assumed name; another name

alibi: the defense by an accused person that he was verifiably elsewhere at the time of the crime with which he is charged.

alien: one born in another country; a foreigner

alter ego: the second self; a substitute or deputy

altruist: a person unselfishly concerned for the welfare of others

allegory: figurative treatment of one subject under the guise of another

Of course, Maurice being Maurice, still managed to find himself in a serious *altercation* with a potential buyer.

AM: love (Latin)

amateur: a person who engages in an activity for pleasure rather than financial or professional gain

amatory: of or pertaining to lovers or lovemaking

amenity: agreeable ways or manners

amorous: inclined to love, esp. sexual love

enamored: inflamed with love; charmed; captivated

amity: friendship; peaceful harmony

inamorata: a female lover

amiable: having or showing agreeable personal qualities

amicable: characterized by exhibiting good will

It turned out however, much to the dealer's relief, that the potential buyer had also been a former *paramour* of Maurice's.

AMB: to go, to walk (Latin)

ambient: moving freely; circulating

ambitious: desirous of achieving or obtaining power

preamble: an introductory statement

ambassador: an authorized messenger or representative

ambulance: a wheeled vehicle equipped for carrying sick people, usually to a hospital

ambulatory: of, pertaining to, or capable of walking

ambush: the act of lying concealed so as to attack by surprise

perambulator: one who makes a tour of inspection on foot

The dealer decided to *amble* over and see if it was possible to smooth things over.

AMB/AMPH: both, more than one, around (Latin)

ambiguous: open to various interpretations

amphibian: any cold-blooded vertebrate, the larva of which are aquatic, and the adult of which are terrestrial; a person or thing having a twofold nature

ambivalent: uncertainty or fluctuation
ambidextrous: able to use both hands equally well

Fortunately, the *ambiance* of the showing was a warm and welcoming one.

ANIM: life, mind, soul, spirit (Latin)
unanimous: in complete accord
animosity: a feeling of ill will or enmity
animus: hostile feeling or attitude
equanimity: mental or emotional stability, especially under tension
magnanimous: generous in forgiving an insult or injury

Maurice became quite *animated* during a conversation with one of the more well-heeled visitors to the gallery.

ANTE: before (Latin)
anterior: placed before
antecedent: existing, being, or going before
antedate: precede in time
antebellum: before the war
antediluvian: belonging to the period before the biblical Flood; a very old or old-fashioned person

Suddenly the dealer was informed that a most prestigious potential client had arrived and was waiting in the *anteroom.*

ANTHRO/ANDR: man, human (Greek)
anthropology: the science that deals with the origins of mankind
android: robot; mechanical man
misanthrope: one who hates humans or mankind
philanderer: one who carries on flirtations
androgynous: being both male and female
androgen: any substance that promotes masculine characteristics
anthropocentric: regarding man as the central fact of the universe

The dealer immediately recognized him as the state's most illustrious *philanthropist.*

ANNUI/ENNI: year (Latin)
annual: of, for, or pertaining to a year; yearly
anniversary: the yearly recurrence of the date of a past event
annuity: a specified income payable at stated intervals
perennial: lasting for an indefinite amount of time
annals: a record of events, esp. a yearly record

"It feels like a *millenium* since we last met," the dealer offered warmly as he shook Mr. Rockebeller's hand.

ANTI: against (Greek)

antibody: a protein naturally existing in blood serum, that reacts to overcome the toxic effects of an antigen

antidote: a remedy for counteracting the effects of poison, disease, etc.

antiseptic: free from germs; especially clean or neat

antipathy: aversion

antipodal: on the opposite side of the globe

"Goodness I hadn't meant to be *antisocial*," Mr. Rockebeller rejoindered.

APO: away (Greek)

apology: an expression of one's regret or sorrow for having wronged another

apostle: one of the 12 disciples sent forth by Jesus to preach the gospel

apocalypse: revelation; discovery; disclosure

apogee: the highest or most distant point

apocryphal: of doubtful authorship or authenticity

apostasy: a total desertion from one's religion, principles, party, cause, etc.

"You are the *apotheosis* of graciousness," the dealer groveled.

ARCH/ARCHI/ARCHY: chief, principal, ruler (Greek)

architect: the devisor, maker, or planner of anything

archenemy: chief enemy

monarchy: a government in which the supreme power is lodged in a sovereign

anarchy: a state or society without government or law

oligarchy: a state or society ruled by a select group

Fortunately they were abruptly interrupted by someone not very high up in the gallery *hierarchy*.

AUTO: self (Greek)

automatic: self-moving or self-acting

autopsy: inspection and dissection of a body after death

autocrat: an absolute ruler

autonomy: independence or freedom

"Help!" the underling cried out. "Maurice is dead. There must be an *autopsy*!" And so the gallery event, came to a close.

BE: to be, to have a particular quality, to exist (Old English)

belittle: to regard something as less impressive than it apparently is

bemoan: to express pity for

bewilder: to confuse or puzzle completely

belie: to misrepresent; to contradict
bemuse: to stupefy (someone)

Abigail was *bemused* by the flirtations of the handsome young man to her right.

BEL/BEL: war (Latin)
antebellum: before the war
rebel: a person who resists authority, control, or tradition
belligerent: warlike, given to waging war
bellicose: inclined or eager to fight

His *bellicosity* belied his charm.

BEN/BON: good (Latin)
benefit: anything advantageous to a person or thing
benign: having a kindly disposition
benediction: act of uttering a blessing
benevolent: desiring to do good to others
bonus: something given over and above what is due
bona fide: in good faith; without fraud

He is either, she thought, a true *bon vivant*, or a *beneficent* man who prefers to hide his good works beneath a tacky exterior.

BI: twice, double (Latin)
binoculars: involving two eyes
biennial: happening every two years
bilateral: pertaining to or affecting two or both sides
bilingual: able to speak one's native language and another with equal facility
bipartisan: representing two parties

"You know," Abigail's friend whispered in her ear, "I have heard he's a *bigamist.*" She paused. "Those poor wives"

CAD/CID: to fall, to happen by chance (Latin)
accident: happening by chance; unexpected
coincidence: a striking occurrence of two or more events at one time apparently by chance
decadent: decaying; deteriorating
cascade: a waterfall descending over a steep surface
recidivist: one who repeatedly relapses, as into crime

Pierre spoke with a lovely *cadence.*

CANT/CENT/CHANT: to sing (Latin)

accent: prominence of a syllable in terms of pronunciation

chant: a song; singing

enchant: to subject to magical influence; bewitch

recant: to withdraw or disavow a statement

incantation: the chanting of words purporting to have magical power

incentive: that which incites action

When the *cantor* stood up to sing even Pierre was struck dumb.

CAP/CIP/CEPT: to take, to get (Latin)

capture: to take by force or stratagem

anticipate: to realize beforehand; foretaste or foresee

susceptible: capable of receiving, admitting, undergoing, or being affected by something

emancipate: to free from restraint

percipient: having perception; discerning; discriminating

precept: a commandment or direction given as a rule of conduct

An *incipient* awe filled the synagogue as the mesmerized congregation listened.

CAP/CAPIT/CIPIT: head, headlong (Latin)

capital: the city or town that is the official seat of government

disciple: one who is a pupil of the doctrines of another

precipitate: to hasten the occurrence of; bring about prematurely

precipice: a cliff with a vertical face

capitulate: to surrender unconditionally or on stipulated terms

caption: a heading or title

Immediately after the service, one woman, acting *precipitously,* threw her arms around the cantor to thank him.

CARD/CORD/COUR: heart (Greek)

cardiac: pertaining to the heart

encourage: to inspire with spirit or confidence

concord: agreement; peace, amity

discord: lack of harmony between persons or things

concordance: agreement, concord, harmony

The cantor was *cordial* in his response, though clearly headed for a coronary.

CARN: flesh (Latin)

carnivorous: that eats flesh

carnage: the slaughter of a great number of people

carnival: a traveling amusement show

reincarnation: rebirth of a soul in a new body
incarnation: a form invested with a bodily form

Though nothing of an intimate *carnal* nature had occurred, Ms. Levinsohn regretted her spontaneous display.

CAST/CHAST: cut (Latin)

cast: to throw or hurl; fling
caste: a hereditary social group, limited to people of the same rank
castigate: to punish in order to correct
chastise: to discipline, esp. by corporal punishment
chaste: free from obscenity; decent

Chastened by the cantor's surprised expression, Ms. Levinsohn determined she would have to control her impulsivity.

CED/CEED/CESS: to go, to yield, to stop (Latin)

antecedent: existing, being, or going before
recede: to go or move away, retreat
concede: to acknowledge as true, just, or proper; admit
predecessor: one who comes before another in an office, position, etc.
cessation: a temporary or complete discontinuance
incessant: without stop

As Ms. Levinsohn strolled home, her embarrassment began to *recede.*

CENTR: center (Greek)

concentrate: to bring to a common center, converge, direct toward one point
eccentric: off center
concentric: having a common center, as circles or spheres
centrifuge: an apparatus that rotates at high speed that separates the substances of different densities using centrifugal force
centrist: of or pertaining to moderate political or social ideas

She'd been accused many times in her life of being *egocentric*, and so had gotten used to the notion that she was often seen in an unflattering light.

CERN/CERT/CRET/CRIM/CRIT: to separate, judge, distinguish, decide (Latin)

discrete: detached from others, separate
ascertain: to find our definitely, determine
certitude: freedom from doubt
discreet: judicious in one's conduct of speech, esp. with regard to maintaining silence about something of a delicate nature
hypocrite: a person who pretends to have beliefs that she does not
criterion: a standard of judgment or criticism

Ms. Levinsohn had also suffered, she knew, the *recriminations* of her tendency to behave as she pleased.

CHRON: time (Latin)
synchronize: to occur at the same time or agree in time
chronology: the sequential order in which past events occurred
anachronism: an obsolete or archaic form
chronic: constant, habitual
chronometer: a time piece with a mechanism to adjust for accuracy

It suddenly occurred to Ms. Levinsohn that to construct a *chronicle* of her constant missteps might help to bring her behavior under control.

CIRUC: around, on all sides (Latin)
circumference: the outer boundary of a circular area
circumstances: the existing conditions or state of affairs surrounding and affecting an agent
circuit: the act of going or moving around
circumambulate: to walk about or around
circuitous: roundabout, not direct

It took many hours, as she had underestimated how difficult it was for her to be *circumspect.*

CIS: to cut (Latin)
scissors: cutting instrument for paper, pieces of cloth, etc.
precise: definitely stated or defined
exorcise: to seek to expel an evil spirit by ceremony
incision: a cut, gash, or notch
incisive: penetrating, cutting

Still, Ms. Levinsohn managed to be *concise* about the wheres, whens and hows.

CLA/CLO/CLU: shut, close (Latin)
conclude: to bring to an end; finish; terminate
claustrophobia: an abnormal fear of enclosed places
disclose: to make known, reveal, or uncover
exclusive: not admitting of something else; shutting out others
cloister: a courtyard bordered with covered walks, esp. in a religious institution *preclude:* to prevent the presence, existence, or occurrence of

Ms. Levinsohn was so horrified at the number of incidents in which she behaved inappropriately, that she considered becoming a *recluse.*

CLAIM/CLAM: to shout, to cry out (Latin)
exclaim: to cry out or speak suddenly and vehemently
proclaim: to announce or declare in an official way
clamor: a loud uproar
disclaim: to deny interest in or connection with
reclaim: to claim or demand the return of a right or possession

She considered calling the people whom she'd offended to *declaim* her guilt.

CLI: to lean toward (Greek)
decline: to cause to slope or incline downward
recline: to lean back
climax: the most intense point in the development of something
proclivity: inclination, bias
disinclination: aversion, distaste

But her *inclination* to think of her own needs first, got in the way.

CO/COL/COM/CON: with, together (Latin)
connect: bind or fasten together
coerce: to compel by force, intimidation, or authority
compatible: capable of existing together in harmony
collide: to strike one another with a forceful impact
collaborate: to work with another, cooperate
conciliate: to placate, win over
commensurate: suitable in measure, proportionate

She simply promised herself that she would be more *congenial* in the future.

CRE/CRESC/CRET: to grow (Latin)
accrue: to be added as a matter of periodic gain
creation: the act of producing or causing to exist
increase: to make greater in any respect
increment: something added or gained; an addition or increase
accretion: an increase by natural growth

Her enthusiasm for this idea reached a *crescendo.*

CRED: to believe, to trust (Latin)
incredible: unbelievable
credentials: anything that provides the basis for belief
credo: any formula of belief
credulity: willingness to believe or trust too readily
credit: trustworthiness

She gave no other life goal any *credence.*

CRYP: hidden (Greek)

crypt: a subterranean chamber or vault
apocryphal: of doubtful authorship or authenticity
cryptology: the science of interpreting secret writings, codes, ciphers, and the like
cryptography: procedures of making and using secret writing

To her few friends, however, she remained *cryptic* about her new approach to life.

CUB/CUMB: to lie down (Latin)

cubicle: any small space or compartment partitioned off
succumb: to give away to superior force; yield
incubate: to sit upon for the purpose of hatching
incumbent: holding an indicated position
recumbent: lying down; reclining; leaning

Ms. Levinsohn shortly thereafter discovered that to be generous all the time was rather *cumbersome.*

CULP: blame (Latin)

culprit: a person guilty for an offense
culpable: deserving blame or censure
inculpate: to charge with fault
mea culpa: through my fault; my fault

She then decided to *exculpate* herself of all wrong doing.

COUR/CUR: running, a course (Latin)

recur: to happen again
curriculum: the regular course of study
courier: a messenger, traveling in haste, bearing news
excursion: a short journey or trip
cursive: handwriting in flowing strokes with the letters joined together
concur: to accord in opinion; agree
incursion: a hostile entrance into a place, especially suddenly
cursory: going rapidly over something; hasty; superficial

Concurrently she enrolled in a course, entitled, "How To Get What You Want Out of Life."

DE: away, off, down, completely, reversal (Latin)

descend: to move from a higher to a lower place
decipher: to make out the meaning; to interpret
defile: to make foul, dirty, or unclean

defame: to attack the good name or reputation of
deferential: respectful; to yield to judgment
delineate: to trace the outline of; sketch or trace in outline

Ginny *deferred* to the director's view.

DEM: people (Greek)

democracy: government by the people
epidemic: affecting at the same time a large number of people, and spreading from person to person
endemic: peculiar to a particular people or locality
pandemic: general, universal
demographics: vital and social statistics of populations

To her, he was a *demagogue.*

DI/DIA: apart, through (Greek)

dialogue: conversation between two or more persons
diagnose: to determine the identity of something from the symptoms
dilate: to make wider or larger; cause to expand
dilatory: inclined to delay or procrastinate
dichotomy: division into two parts, kinds, etc.

Ginny slipped on the *diaphanous* gown, hoping to finally garner his full attention.

DIC/DICT/DIT: to say, tell, use words (Latin)

dictionary: a book containing a selection of the words of a language
predict: to tell in advance
verdict: judgment, decree
indite: to compose or write, as in a speech
interdict: to forbid. prohibit

But he merely told her to move stage left, a direction she did not dare *contradict.*

DIGN: worth (Latin)

dignity: nobility or elevation of character; worthiness
dignitary: a person who holds a high rank or office
deign: to think fit or in accordance with one's dignity
condign: well deserved; fitting; adequate
disdain: to look upon or treat with contempt

Anxious to appear *dignified,* she moved to the spot with deliberate grace.

DIS/DIF: away from, apart, reversal, not (Latin)
disperse: to drive or send off in various directions
disseminate: to scatter or spread widely; promulgate
dissipate: to scatter wastefully
dissuade: to deter by advice or persuasion
diffuse: to pour out and spread, as a fluid

Ginny wished to *disassociate* herself from the other less talented players.

DAC/DOC: to teach (Latin)
doctor: someone licensed to practice medicine; a learned person
doctrine: a particular principle advocated, as of a government or religion
indoctrinate: to imbue a person with learning
docile: easily managed or handled; tractable
didactic: intended for instruction

She had *documentation* attesting to her great promise, after all.

DOG/DOX: opinion (Greek)
orthodox: sound or correct in opinion or doctrine
paradox: an opinion or statement contrary to accepted opinion
dogma: a system of tenets, as of a church
dogmatic: asserting opinions in an arrogant manner

Ginny was resolved to be *dogged* in her quest for fame.

DOL: suffer, pain (Latin)
condolence: expression of sympathy with one who is suffering
indolence: a state of being lazy, slothful
doleful: sorrowful, mournful
dolorous: full of pain or sorrow, grievous

Ginny occasionally suffered from *doldrums* though, as success was not exactly knocking on her door.

DON/DOT/DOW: to give (Latin)
donate: to present as a gift or contribution
pardon: kind indulgence, forgiveness
antidote: something that prevents or counteracts ill effects
anecdote: a short narrative about an interesting event
endow: to provide with a permanent fund

Her best role so far had been that of a young *dowager* in some Noel Coward—like play.

DUB: doubt (Latin)
dubious: doubtful
dubiety: doubtfulness
indubitable: unquestionable

> Ginny would not allow *doubtfulness* into her consciousness.

DUC/DUCT: to lead (Latin)
abduct: to carry off or lead away
conduct: personal behavior, way of acting
conducive: contributive, helpful
induce: to lead or move by influence
induct: to install in a position with formal ceremonies
produce: to bring into existence; give cause to

> She would not allow herself to feel *reduced* by small roles.

DUR: hard (Latin)
endure: to hold out against, sustain without yielding
durable: able to resist decay
duress: compulsion by threat, coercion
dour: sullen, gloomy
during: throughout the continuance, or existence of
duration: the length of time something exists

> Ginny only grew *obdurate* when asked to interpret a line incorrectly.

DYS: faulty, abnormal (Greek)
dystrophy: faulty or inadequate nutrition or development
dyspepsia: deranged or impaired digestion
dyslexia: an impairment of the ability to read due to a brain defect
dysfunctional: malfunctioning

> Ginny did however suffer from constant *dysphoria*, in particular when playing a role she would not admit was beneath her—which was just about always.

EPI: upon (Greek)
epidemic: affecting at the same time a large number of people, and spreading from person to person
epilogue: a concluding part added to a literary work
epidermis: the outer layer of the skin
epigram: a witty or pointed saying tersely expressed
epithet: a word, phrase, used invectively as a term of abuse

> George was the *epitome* of handsomeness.

EQU: equal, even (Latin)

equation: the act of making equal

adequate: equal to the requirement or occasion

equilibrium: a state of rest or balance due to the equal action of opposing forces

equidistant: equally distant

iniquity: gross injustice; wickedness

Women had trouble keeping their *equilibrium* when he entered the room.

ERR: to wander (Latin)

err: to go astray in thought or belief, to be mistaken

error: a deviation from accuracy or correctness

erratic: deviating from the proper or usual course in conduct

arrant: downright, thorough, notorious

erroneous: containing error

In fact they often exhibited *aberrant* behavior around him.

ESCE: becoming (Latin)

adolescent: between childhood and adulthood

obsolescent: becoming obsolete

incandescent: glowing with heat, shining

convalescent: recovering from illness

reminiscent: reminding or suggestive of

June, an aggressive woman, for example, would become quite *acquiescent*.

EU: good, well (Greek)

euphoria: intense sense of well being and excitement

eulogy: speech or writing in praise or commendation

eugenics: improvement of qualities of race by control of inherited characteristics

euthanasia: killing person painlessly, especially one who has incurable painful disease

euphony: pleasantness of sound

A *euphemism* is a word that covers up something unpleasant.

E/EF/EX: out, out of, from, former, completely (Latin)

evade: escape from, avoid

exclude: shut out, leave out

extricate: disentangle, release

exonerate: free or declare free from blame

expire: come to an end, cease to be valid
efface: rub or wipe out; surpass, eclipse

She would of course *exhort* George to be kind, warm, loving.

EXTRA: outside of beyond (Latin)

extraordinary: beyond the ordinary
extract: take out, obtain against person's will
extradite: hand over (person accused of crime) to state where crime was committed
extrasensory: derived by means other than known senses
extrapolate: estimate (unknown facts or values) from known data

But George clearly viewed June as *extraneous.* And so that was that.

FAB/FAM: speak (Latin)

fable: fictional tale, esp. legendary
affable: friendly, courteous
ineffable: too great for description in words; that must not be uttered
famous: well known, celebrated
defame: attack good name of

Lola was an *infamous* liar.

FAC/FIC/FIG/FAIT/FEIT/FY: to do, to make (French)

factory: building for manufacture of goods
faction: small dissenting group within larger one, especially in politics
deficient: incomplete or insufficient
prolific: producing many offspring or much output
configuration: manner of arrangement, shape
ratify: confirm or accept by formal consent
effigy: sculpture or model of person
counterfeit: imitation, forgery

She was quite *facile* when it came to uttering falsehoods.

FER: to bring, to carry, to bear (Latin)

offer: present for acceptance, refusal, or consideration
confer: grant, bestow
referendum: vote on political question open to entire electorate
proffer: to offer
proliferate: reproduce; produce rapidly

She could be *vociferous* too, especially when the lie was an important one.

FERV: to boil, to bubble (Latin)
  fervor: passion, zeal
  fervid: ardent, intense
  effervescent: with the quality of giving off bubbles of gas

> Then again, Lola was also quite *fervent* when speaking the truth.

FID: faith, trust (Latin)
  confide: to entrust with a secret
  affidavit: written statement on oath
  fidelity: faithfulness, loyalty
  fiduciary: of a trust; held or given in trust
  infidel: disbeliever in especially the supposed true religion

> She had but one *confidant* with whom she was always honest.

FIN: end (French)
  final: at the end, coming last
  confine: keep or restrict within certain limits; imprison
  definitive: decisive, unconditional, final
  infinite: boundless; endless
  infinitesimal: infinitely or very small

> Lola felt a strange *affinity* for Brigitte.

FLAG/FLAM: to burn (French)
  flame: ignited gas
  flammable: easily set on fire
  flambeau: a lighted torch
  flagrant: blatant, scandalous
  conflagration: large destructive fire

> Brigitte could be quite *flamboyant*.

FLECT/FLEX: to bend (Latin)
  deflect: bend or turn aside from purpose
  flexible: able to bend without breaking
  inflect: change or vary pitch of
  reflect: throw back
  genuflect: bend knee, esp. in worship

> She also spoke with an odd *inflection*.

FLU/FLUX: to flow (Latin)
  fluid: substance, esp. gas or liquid, capable of flowing freely
  fluctuation: something which varies, rises and falls
  effluence: flowing out of (light, electricity, etc.)

confluence: merging into one
mellifluous: pleasing, musical

> She wore diamonds everywhere, as if to announce her *affluence*.

FORE: before   (English)

foresight: care or provision for future
foreshadow: be warning or indication of (future event)
forestall: prevent by advance action
forgo: go without, relinquish
forbear: abstain or refrain from

> Lola could *foretell* that Brigitte was headed for trouble.

FORT: chance   (Latin)

fortune: chance or luck in human affairs
fortunate: lucky, auspicious
fortuitous: happening by chance

> It was, Lola believed, *fortuitous* that they met.

FORT: strength   (French)

fortify: provide with fortifications; strengthen
fortissimo: very loud
forthright: straightforward, outspoken, decisive

> but it was *fortitude* that kept them together as they really had nothing significant in common.

FRA/FRAC/FRAG/FRING: to break   (Latin)

fracture: breakage, esp. of a bone
fragment: a part broken off
fractious: irritable, peevish
refractory: stubborn, unmanageable, rebellious
infringe: break or violate (law, etc.)

> In fact their relationship might have *fractured* years ago if it wasn't for one important thing.

FUS: to pour   (Latin)

profuse: lavish, extravagant, copious
fusillade: continuous discharge of firearms or outburst of criticism
suffuse: spread throughout or over from within
diffuse: spread widely or thinly
infusion: infusing, liquid extract so obtained

> Brigitte and Lola share the same blood type, which was fortunate because when Lola needed a *transfusion*, Britte volunteered a pint, earning *effusive* praise from her new best friend.

GEN: birth, creation, race, kind (Latin)

generous: giving or given freely
genetics: study of heredity and variation among animals and plants
gender: classification roughly corresponding to the two sexes and sexlessness
carcinogenic: substance producing cancer
congenital: existing or as such from birth
progeny: offspring, descendants
miscegenation: interbreeding of races

Walter was a *genial* little fellow.

GN/GNO: know (Latin)

agnostic: person who believes that existence of God is not provable
ignore: refuse to take notice of
ignoramus: a person lacking knowledge, uninformed
recognize: identify as already known
incognito: with one's name or identity concealed
prognosis: forecast, especially of disease
diagnose: make an identification of disease or fault from symptoms

His *cognitive* powers were advanced for his age.

GRAT: pleasing (Latin)

grateful: thankful
ingratiate: bring oneself into favor
gratuity: money given for good service
graciousness: kindly, esp. to inferiors; merciful

Still, one day he was accused of being an *ingrate*.

GRAD/GRESS: to step (Latin)

progress: forward movement
aggressive: given to hostile act or feeling
degrade: humiliate, dishonor, reduce to lower rank
digress: depart from main subject
egress: going out; way out

This caused him to *regress*, ultimately resulting in his inability to read until the age of ten.

HER/HES: to stick (Latin)

coherent: logically consistent; having waves in phase and of one wavelength
adhesive: tending to remain in memory; sticky; an adhesive substance
inherent: involved in the constitution or essential character of something
adherent: able to adhere; believer or advocate of a particular thing

heredity: the qualities genetically derived from one's ancestors, the transmission of those qualities

The figure skating club was a **cohesive** group

(H)ETERO: different (Greek)
heterosexual: sexual orientation toward members of the opposite sex; relating to different sexes
heterogeneous: of other origin: not originating in the body
heterodox: different from acknowledged standard; holding unorthodox opinions or doctrines

The *heterogeneity* of the members oddly enough contributed to the harmony

(H)OM: same (Greek)
homogeneous: of the same or a similar kind of nature; of uniform structure of composition throughout
homonym: one of two or more words spelled and pronounced alike but different in meaning
homosexual: of, relating to, or exhibiting sexual desire toward a member of one's own sex
anomaly: deviation from the common rule
homeostasis: a relatively stable state of equilibrium

The club physician practices *homeopathy* which is the practice of using minute dosages of remedy to produce the same symptoms of the disease being treated.

HYPER: over, excessive (Greek)
hyperactive: excessively active
hyperbole: extravagant exaggeration used as a figure of speech

HYPO: under, beneath, less than (Greek)
hypodermic: relating to the parts beneath the skin
hypochondriac: one affected by extreme depression of mind or spirits often centered on imaginary physical ailments
hypocritical: to affect virtues or qualities she or he does not have

Of course the *hypothesis* of the club members as to why they get along is simply that when it comes to skating they are each hyperactive.

ID: one's own (Latin)
idiot: an utterly stupid person
idiom: a language, dialect, or style of speaking particular to a people
idiosyncrasy: a characteristic, habit, mannerism that is distinctive of an individual

ideology: the body of doctrine that guides an individual, social movement, institution, or group

Paris had no *identity* of his own.

IM/IN/EM/EN: in, into (Latin)

embrace: to clasp in the arms; to include or contain
enclose: to close in on all sides
intrinsic: belonging to a thing by its very nature
influx: the act of flowing in; inflow
implicit: not expressly stated; implied
incarnate: given a bodily, esp. a human, form.
indigenous: native; innate, natural

Paris would attempt to *ingratiate* himself by behaving in ways he felt others would approve.

IM/IN: not, without (Latin)

inactive: not active
innocuous: not harmful or injurious
indolence: showing a disposition to avoid exertion; slothful
impartial: not partial or biased; just
indigent: deficient in what is requisite

He would occasionally suffer *indignities* because of this approach.

INTER: between, among (Latin)

interstate: connecting or jointly involving states
interim: a temporary or provisional arrangement; meantime
interloper: one who intrudes in the domain of others
intermittent: stopping or ceasing for a time
intersperse: to scatter here and there

When asked, "Don't you have an original thought? Don't you think." Paris would quickly *interject* "Yes! Of course. What do you think?"

JECT: to throw, to throw down (Latin)

inject: place (quality, etc.) where needed in something
dejected: sad, depressed
eject: throw out, expel
conjecture: formation of opinion on incomplete information
abject: utterly hopeless, humiliating, or wretched

Blaine's arrow followed a dangerous *trajectory.*

JOIN/JUNCT: to meet, to join (Latin)
junction: the act of joining; combining
adjoin: to be next to and joined with
subjugate: to conquer
rejoinder: reply, retort
junta: (usually military) clique taking power after a *coup d'etat.*

Her *conjugal* relationship, you see, was unsatisfactory.

JUR: to swear (Latin)
perjury: willful lying while on oath
abjure: renounce on oath
adjure: to beg or command

This is why she ended up in front of a *jury.*

LECT/LEG: to select, to choose (Latin)
collect: to gather together, assemble
elect: choose, decide
select: to choose with care
electorate: group of people entitled to vote in an election
eclectic: selecting ideas, etc. from various sources

Midge had a *predilection* for tall men.

LEV: lift, light, rise (Latin)
relieve: to mitigate the tedium of
alleviate: to make easier to endure, lessen
relevant: bearing on or pertinent to information at hand
levee: embankment against river flooding

Her friends noted this fact with considerable *levity.*

LOC/LOG/LOQU: word, speech (Latin)
dialogue: conversation, esp. in a literary work
elocution: art of clear and expressive speaking
prologue: introduction to poem, play, etc.
eulogy: speech or writing in praise of consideration
colloquial: of ordinary or familiar conversation
grandiloquent: pompous or inflated in language

Whenever Midge saw a tall man, she would amble over and immediately display a scintillating and *loquacious* side.

LUC/LUM/LUS: light (Latin)
illustrate: to make intelligible with examples or analogies
illuminate: to supply or brighten with light

illustrious: highly distinguished
translucent: permitting light to pass through
lackluster: lacking brilliance or radiance
lucid: easily understood, intelligible

Her countenance would in fact become *luminous*.

LUD/LUS: to play (Latin)

allude: to refer casually or indirectly
illusion: something hat deceives by producing a false impression of reality
ludicrous: ridiculous, laughable
delude: to mislead the mind or judgment of, deceive
elude: to avoid capture or escape defection by
prelude: a preliminary to an action, event, etc.

Ultimately the conversation would lead to a romantic *interlude*.

LUT/LUT/LUV: to wash (Latin)

lavatory: a room with equipment for washing hands and face
dilute: to make thinner or weaker by the addition of water
pollute: to make foul or unclean
deluge: a great flood of water
antediluvian: before the biblical flood; extremely old

Afterwards Midge would engage in a ritual *ablution*, so as to be ready for her next tall paramour.

MAG/MAJ/ MAX: big (Latin)

magnify: to increase the apparent size of
magnitude: greatness of size, extent, or dimensions
maximum: the highest amount, value, or degree attained
magnanimous: generous in forgiving an insult or injury
maxim: an expression of general truth or principle

C. J. Warner's *magniloquent* manner put off all of his employees.

MAL/MALE: bad, ill, evil, wrong (Latin)

malfunction: failure to function properly
malicious: full of or showing malice
malign: to speak harmful untruths about, to slander
malady: a disorder or disease of the body
malfeasance: misconduct or wrongdoing committed esp. by a public official
malediction: a curse

Of course his *malodorousness*, which made it difficult to stand near him, didn't help.

MAN: hand (Latin)

manual: operated by hand
manufacture: to make by hand or machinery
emancipate: free from bondage
manifest: readily perceived by the eye or the understanding
mandate: an authoritative order or command

Oddly however, C. J. Warner considered it *mandatory* that each of his employees wear cologne.

MIN: small (Latin)

minute: a unit of time equal to one-sixtieth of an hour, or sixty seconds.
minutiae: a small or trivial detail
miniature: a copy or model that represents something in greatly reduced size
diminish: to lessen
diminution: the act or process of diminishing

A *minimal* amount would do.

MIN: to project, to hang over (Latin)

eminent: towering above others; projecting
imminent: about to occur; impending
prominent: projecting outward
preeminent: superior to or notable above all others

Still, no matter how he or his employees smelled, C. J. had a *minatory* effect on everyone he met.

MIS/MIT: to send (Latin)

transmit: to send from one person, thing, or place to another
emissary: a messenger or agent sent to represent the interests of another
intermittent: stopping and starting at intervals
remit: to send money
remission: a lessening of intensity or degree

It's safe to say all who worked for C. J. prayed for his *demise.*

MISC: mixed (Latin)

miscellaneous: made up of a variety of parts or ingredients
miscegenation: the interbreeding of races, especially marriage between white and nonwhite persons
promiscuous: consisting of diverse and unrelated parts or individuals

While it is true that emotions are generally *miscible,* when it came to the staff of C. J. Warner there were no mixed feelings.

MON/MONIT: to remind, warn (Latin)
monument: a structure, such as a building, tower, or sculpture, erected as a memorial
monitor: one that admonishes, cautions, or reminds
summons: to call together; convene
admonish: to counsel against something; caution
remonstrate: to say or plead in protect, objection, or reproof

C. J. himself had a *premonition* one day.

MORPH: shape (Greek)
amorphous: without definite form; lacking a specific shape
metamorphosis: a transformation, as by magic or sorcery
anthropomorphic: attribution of human characteristics to inanimate objects, animals, or natural phenomena

C. J. went from being an *endomorphi* to an *ectomorph* within a few weeks.

MORT: death (French)
immortal: not subject to death
morgue: a place in which dead bodies are kept for identification and arrangement of burial
morbid: susceptible to preoccupation with unwholesome matters
moratorium: a deferment or delay of any action
moribund: at the point of death

He grew *moribund* shortly thereafter.

MUT: change (Latin)
commute: to substitute; exchange; interchange
mutation: the process of being changed
transmutation: the act of changing from one form into another
permutation: a complete change; transformation

Upon his death it was agreed that C. J. was better off, as he was *immutable,* and would have driven everyone crazy forever.

NAM/NOM/NOUN/NOWN/NYM: rule, order (Greek)
acronym: a word formed from the initial letters of a name
astronomy: the scientific study of the universe beyond the earth
economy: the careful or thrifty use of resources, as of income, materials, or labor
gastronomy: the art or science of good eating
taxonomy: the science, laws, or principles of classification

Beatrix loved her *autonomy.*

NAT/NAS/NAI: to be born (Latin)

natural: present due to nature, not to artificial or man-made means
native: belonging to one by nature; inborn; innate
naive: lacking worldliness and sophistication; artless
cognate: related by blood; having a common ancestor
renaissance: rebirth, especially referring to culture

At four years old she had an *innate* sense of her own power.

NEC/NIC/NOC/ NOX: harm, death (Latin)

innocent: uncorrupted by evil, malice, or wrongdoing
noxious: injurious or harmful to health or morals
obnoxious: highly disagreeable or offensive
innocuous: having no adverse effect; harmless
necromancy: black magic

Nicole could also be a tad *pernicious* in her demands.

NOM/NYM/NOUN/NOWN: name (Greek)

synonym: a word having a meaning similar to that of another word of the
same language
anonymous: having an unknown or unacknowledged name
nominate: to propose by name as a candidate
nomenclature: a system of names; systematic naming
acronym: a word formed from the initial letters of a name

She was, in fact, becoming somewhat *ignominious* in her play group,
as she had a nasty habit of grabbing toys.

NOVE/NEO/ NOU: new (Latin)

novice: a person new to any field or activity
renovate: to restore to an earlier condition
innovate: to begin or introduce something new
neologism: a newly coined word, phrase, or expression
neophyte: a recent convert
nouveau riche: one who has lately become rich

Hers was a *novel* technique.

NOUNC/NUNC: to announce (Latin)

announce: to proclaim
pronounce: to articulate
renounce: to give up, especially by formal announcement

She would *denounce* the other four-year-olds in her group and
declare the toys hers for safe-keeping until they mended their ways.

OB/OC/OF/OP: toward, to, against, completely, over (Latin)
obese: extremely fat, corpulent
obstinate: stubbornly adhering to an idea, inflexible
obstruct: to block or fill with obstacles
oblique: having a slanting or sloping direction
obstreperous: noisily defiant, unruly
obtuse: not sharp, pointed, or acute in any form
obfuscate: to render indistinct or dim; darken

Jeremy was *obsequious* in the presence of his spiritual leader.

OMNI: all (Latin)
omnibus: an anthology of the works of one author or of writings on related subjects
omnipresent: everywhere at one time
omnipotent: all powerful

His leader, he was convinced, had great powers of *omniscience*.

PAC/PEAC: peace (Latin)
appease: to bring peace to
pacify: to ease the anger or agitation of
pacifier: something or someone which eases the anger or agitation of
pact: a formal agreement, as between nations

George considered himself a *pacifist*.

PAN: all everyone (Greek)
panorama: an unobstructed and wide view of an extensive area
panegyric: formal or elaborate praise at an assembly
panoply: a wide-ranging and impressive array or display
pantheon: a public building containing tombs or memorials of the illustrious dead of a nation *pandemic:* widespread, general, universal

The *pandemonium* that typically accompanies war, made him cringe.

PAR: equal (Latin)
par: an equality in value or standing
parity: equally, as in amount, status, or character
apartheid: any system or caste that separates people according to race, etc.
disparate: essentially different

He *disparaged* all those who supported aggressive action overseas.

PARA: next to, beside (Greek)
parallel: extending in the same direction
parasite: an organism that lives on or within a plant or animal of another

species, from which it obtains nutrients

parody: to imitate for purposes of satire

parable: a short allegorical story designed to illustrate a moral lesson or religious principle

paragon: a model of excellence

paranoid: suffering from a baseless distrust of others

George's best friend joined the *paramilitary* mistakenly assuming he would never see battle.

PAS/PAT/ PATH: feeling, suffering, disease (Greek)

sympathy: harmony or of agreement in feeling

empathy: the identification with the feelings or thoughts of others

compassion: a feeling of deep sympathy for someone struck by misfortune, accompanied by a desire to alleviate the suffering

dispassionate: devoid of personal feeling or bias

impassive: showing or feeling no emotion

sociopath: a person whose behavior is antisocial and who lacks a sense of moral responsibility

He was badly hurt in action which only served to fuel George's *antipathy* for war.

PO/POV/PAU/PU: few, little, poor (Latin)

poor: having little or no money, goods, or other means of support

poverty: the condition of being poor

paucity: smallness of quantity; scarcity; scantiness

pauper: a person without any personal means of support

impoverish: to deplete

puerile: youthful, juvenile

pusillanimous: lacking courage or resolution

George could become quite *puerile* when discussing his views.

PED: child, education (Greek)

pedagogue: a teacher

pediatrician: a doctor who primarily has children as patients

encyclopedia: book or set of books containing articles on various topics, covering all branches of knowledge or of one particular subject

He would behave as if he belonged on a pedestal and become quite *petulant* when others did not appear to admire him.

PED/POD: foot (Greek)

pedal: a foot-operated lever or part used to control

pedestrian: a person who travels on foot

expedite: to speed up the progress of
impede: to retard progress by means of obstacles or hindrances
podium: a small platform for an orchestra conductor, speaker, etc.
antipodes: places diametrically opposite each other on the globe

George had many *impediments* to his happiness.

PEN/PUN: to pay, or compensate (Latin)
penal: of or pertaining to punishment, as for crimes
penalty: a punishment imposed for a violation of law or rule
punitive: serving for, concerned with, or inflicting punishment
penance: a punishment undergone to express regret for a sin
penitent: contrite
repine: to fret or complain

But he continued to think he could rail at others with *impunity.*

PEND/PENS: to hang, to weight, to pay (Latin)
depend: to rely, place trust
stipend: a periodic payment; fixed or regular pay
compensate: to counterbalance, offset
indispensable: absolutely necessary, essential, or requisite
appendix: supplementary material at the end of a text
appendage: a limb or other subsidiary part that diverges from the central structure

Finally the *pendulum* began to swing in another direction.

PER: completely, wrong (Latin)
persistent: lasting or enduring tenaciously
perforate: to make a way through or into something
perplex: to cause to be puzzled or bewildered over what is not understood
peruse: to read with thoroughness or care
perfunctory: performed merely as routine duty
pertinacious: resolute

Natalie, a *perspicacious* young woman, entered his life and quickly got the picture.

PERI: around (Greek)
perimeter: the border or outer boundary of a two-dimensional figure
periscope: an optical instrument for seeing objects in an obstructed field of vision
peripheral: concerned with the superficial aspects of a question
peripatetic: walking or traveling about; itinerant

George, she realized, had only a *peripheral* understanding of his own beliefs.

PET/PIT: to go, to seek, to strive (Latin)
appetite: a desire of food or drink
compete: to strive to outdo another for acknowledgment
petition: a formally drawn request soliciting some benefit
impetuous: characterized by sudden or rash action or emotion
petulant: showing sudden irritation, esp. over some annoyance

Natalie decided this was a *propitious* time to determine what was really bothering George.

PHIL: love (Greek)
philosophy: the rational investigation of the truths and principles of being, knowledge, or conduct
philatelist: one who loves or collects postage
philology: the study of literary texts to establish their authenticity and determine their meaning
bibliophile: one who loves or collects books

He seemed honest and so Natalie did not suspect George of being a *philanderer.*

PLAC: to please (Latin)
placid: pleasantly calm or peaceful
placebo: a substance which has no pharmacological effect but which acts to placate a patient who believes it to be a medicine
implacable: unable to be pleased
complacent: self-satisfied, unconcerned
complaisant: inclined or disposed to please

Natalie, not even slightly interested in *placating* George, simply asked "What's really bugging you? It can't just be war."

PLE: to fill (Latin)
complete: having all parts or elements
deplete: to decrease seriously or exhaust the supply of
supplement: something added to supply a deficiency
implement: an instrument, tool, or utensil for accomplishing work
replete: abundantly supplied

George sighed and replied, "I suppose there are a *plethora* of reasons for my rage."

PLEX/PLIC/PLY: to fold, to twist, to tangle, to bend (Latin)
complex: composed of many interconnected parts
replica: any close copy or reproduction

implicit: not expressly stated, implied

implicate: to show to be involved, usually in an incriminating manner

duplicity: deceitfulness in speech or conduct, double-dealing *supplicate:* to make humble and earnest entreaty

> He lowered his head and added, "I choose not to be too *explicit*."

PON/POS/ POUND: to put, to place (Latin)

component: a constituent part, elemental ingredient

expose: to lay open to danger, attack, or harm

expound: to set forth in detail

juxtapose: to place close together or side by side, esp. for contract

proponent: a person who puts forward a proposition or proposal

repository: a receptacle or place where things are deposited

> "I am a *proponent* of speaking honestly," Natalie replied encouragingly.

PORT: to carry (Latin)

import: to bring in from a foreign country

export: to transmit abroad

portable: easily carried

deportment: conduct, behavior

disport: to divert or amuse oneself

importune: to urge or press with excessive persistence

> "You *purport* to be a pacifist but I suspect there is more than just that at work."

POST: after (Latin)

posthumous: after death

posterior: situated at the rear of

posterity: succeeding in future generations collectively

post facto: after the fact

> "Well it's certainly not *postpartum* depression," he joked.

PRE: before (Latin)

precarious: dependent on circumstances beyond one's control

precocious: unusually advanced or mature in mental development or talent

premonition: a feeling of anticipation over a future event

presentiment: foreboding

precedent: an act that serves as an example for subsequent situations

precept: a commandment given as a rule of action or conduct

> "My *prerequisite* for helping you face your true problems," Natalie responded haughtily, "is no pathetic jokes."

PREHEND/PRISE: to take, to get, to seize (Latin)
surprise: to strike with an unexpected feeling of wonder or astonishment
enterprise: a project undertaken
reprehensible: deserving rebuke or censure
comprise: to include or contain
reprisals: retaliation against an enemy
apprehend: to take into custody

"Fine, go ahead" George smiled, "Conduct a *comprehensive* investigation into my psyche."

PRO: much, for, a lot (Latin)
prolific: highly fruitful
profuse: spending or giving freely
prodigal: wastefully or recklessly extravagant
prodigious: extraordinary in size, amount, extent
proselytize: to convert or attempt to recruit
propound: to set forth for consideration
provident: having or showing foresight

"*Providence* at work," Natalie replied dryly, "I just received the text for Psychology 101 in the mail."

PROB: to prove, to test (Latin)
probe: to search or examine thoroughly
approbation: praise, consideration
opprobrium: the disgrace incurred by shameful conduct
reprobate: a depraved or wicked person
problematic: questionable

"I will participate with *probity*," George answered sarcastically.

PUG: to fight (Latin)
pug: a boxer
pugnacious: to quarrel or fight readily
impugn: to challenge as false
repugnant: objectionable or offensive

"I believe you are turning into a *pugilist*," Natalie snapped.

PUNC/PUNG/POIGN: to point, to prick (Latin)
point: a sharp or tapering end
puncture: the act of piercing
pungent: caustic or sharply expressive
compunction: a feeling of uneasiness for doing wrong

punctilious: strict or exact in the observance of formalities

"*Expunge* that thought from your mind," George shook is head angrily. "I, perhaps you have forgotten, am a pacifist."

QUE/QUIS: to seek (Latin)
acquire: to come into possession of
exquisite: of special beauty or charm
conquest: vanquishment
inquisitive: given to research, eager for knowledge
query: a question, inquiry
querulous: full of complaints
perquisite: a gratuity, tip

Jane made an *acquisition* of which she is quite proud.

QUI: quiet (Latin)
quiet: making little or no sound
disquiet: lack of calm or peace
tranquil: free from commotion or tumult
acquiesce: to comply, give in
quiescence: the condition of being at rest, still, inactive

The log cabin has given her a long sought feeling of *tranquillity.*

RID/RIS: to laugh (Latin)
riddle: a conundrum
derision: the act of mockery
risible: causing laughter

Paulette was subjected to *ridicule* when she arrived late and sloppy.

ROG: to ask (Latin)
interrogate: to ask questions of, esp. formally
arrogant: making claims to superior importance or rights
prerogative: a right limited to a specific person or persons
abrogate: to abolish by formal means
surrogate: a person appointed to act for another
derogatory: belittling, disparaging
arrogate: to claim unwarrantably or presumptuously

"It is my *prerogative* to arrive when and wear what I please," she responded.

SAL/SIL/SAULT/SULT: to leap, to jump (Latin)
insult: to spread with contemptuous rudeness
assault: a sudden or violent attack

somersault: to roll the body end over end making a complete revolution
salient: prominent or conspicuous
resilient: able to spring back to an original form after compression
insolent: boldly rude or disrespectful
desultory: lacking in consistency, method, or visible order
exult: to show or feel triumphant joy

Harrison moved in a *desultory* fashion from career to career, never really growing interested in anything.

SACR/SANCT/SECR: sacred (Latin)

sacred: devoted or dedicated to a deity or religious purpose
sacrifice: the offering of some living or inanimate thing to a deity in homage
sanctify: to make holy
sanction: authoritative permission or approval
execrable: abominable
sacrament: something regarded as possessing sacred character
sacrilege: the violation of anything sacred

He took *sanctuary* from his relentless meandering, in his writing.

SCI: to know (Latin)

conscious: aware of one's own existence
conscience: the inner sense of what is right or wrong, impelling one toward right action
unconscionable: unscrupulous
omniscient: to know everything
prescient: to have knowledge of things before they happen

Harrison wrote *conscientiously* in his diary every day.

SCRIBE/SCRIP: to write (Latin)

scribble: to write hastily or carelessly
describe: to tell or depict in words, give an account of
script: handwriting
postscript: any addition or supplement
proscribe: to condemn as harmful or odious
ascribe: to credit or assign, as to a cause or course
conscription: draft
transcript: to make a written or typed copy of
circumscribe: to draw a line around

One day, because his hand was tired, he decided to hire a *scribe*.

SE: apart (Latin)

select: to choose in preference to another
separate: to keep apart, divide

seduce: to lead astray
segregate: to separate or set apart from others
secede: to withdraw formally from an association
sequester: to remove or withdraw into solitude or retirement
sedition: incitement of discontent or rebellion against a government

The *scribe* needed to work in *seclusion.*

SEC/SEQU: to follow (Latin)
second: next after the first
prosecute: to seek to enforce by legal process
sequence: the following of one thing after another
obsequious: fawning
non sequitur: an inference or a conclusion that does not follow from the premises

Harrison did not view this as *inconsequential.*

SED/SESS/SID: to sit, to be, still, to plan, to plot (Latin)
preside: to exercise management or control
resident: a person who lives in a place
sediment: the matter that settles to the bottom of a liquid
dissident: disagreeing, as in opinion or attitude
residual: remaining, leftover
subsidiary: serving to assist or supplement
insidious: intended to entrap or beguile

He was *assiduous* about word usage and wanted to be sure the scribe worked with care.

SENS/SENT: to feel, to be, aware (Latin)
sense: any of the faculties by which humans and animals perceive stimuli originating outside the body
sensory: of or pertaining to the senses or sensation
sentiment: an attitude or feeling toward something
presentiment: a feeling that something is about to happen
dissent: to differ in opinion, esp. from the majority
resent: to feel or show displeasure
sentinel: a person or thing that stands watch
insensate: without feeling or sensitivity

Harrison expressed his feeling creating *dissent* between himself and his hired scribe.

SOL: to loosen, to free (Latin)
dissolve: to make a solution of, as by mixing in a liquid
soluble: capable of being dissolved or liquefied

resolution: a formal expression of opinion or intention made
dissolution: the act or process of dissolving into parts or elements
dissolute: indifferent to moral restraints
absolution: forgiveness for wrong-doing

Both were *irresolute* as to what decision should follow.

SPEC/SPIC/SPIT: to look, to see (Latin)

perspective: one's mental view of facts, ideas, and their interrelationships
speculation: the contemplation or consideration of some subject
suspicious: inclined to suspect
spectrum: a broad range of related things that form a continuous series
retrospective: contemplative of past situations
circumspect: watchful and discreet, cautious
perspicacious: having keen mental perception and understanding
conspicuous: easily seen or noticed, readily observable

The scribe growing frustrated with their indecision accused Harrison of hiring him for *specious* reasons.

STA/STI: to stand, to be in place (Latin)

static: of bodies or forces at rest or in equilibrium
destitute: without means of subsistence
obstinate: stubbornly adhering to a purpose, opinion, or course of action
constitute: to make up
stasis: the state of equilibrium or inactivity caused by opposing equal forces
apostasy: renunciation of an object of one's previous loyalty

Harrison *stalwartly* insisted that he had hired him with the purest of intentions but that he simply wanted to stand over the scribe's shoulder as he worked.

SUA: smooth (Latin)

suave: smoothly agreeable or polite
persuade: to encourage, convince
dissuade: to deter

This did not *assuage* the scribe's fury.

SUB/SUP: below (Latin)

submissive: inclined or ready to submit
subsidiary: serving to assist or supplement
subliminal: existing or operating below the threshold of confidence
subtle: thin, tenuous, or rarefied
subterfuge: an artifice or expedient used to evade a rule
supposition: the act of assuming

Harrison could not longer *suppress* his annoyance.

SUPER/SUR: above (Latin)

surpass: to go beyond in amount, extent, or degree
superlative: the highest kind or order
supersede: to replace in power, as by another person or thing
surmount: to get over or across, to prevail
surveillance: a watch kept over someone or something

"I do not need you," he announced in a *supercilious* tone, "as you are *superfluous* to my one, joyful endeavor. I shall manage on my own."

TAC/TIC: to be silent (Latin)

reticent: disposed to be silent or not to speak freely
tacit: unspoken understanding

Herman seemed so *taciturn* that few sought his company.

TAIN/TEN/TENT/TIN: to hold (Latin)

detain: to keep from proceeding
pertain: to have reference or relation
tenacious: holding fast
abstention: the act of refraining voluntarily
tenure: the holding or possessing of anything
tenable: capable of being held, maintained, or defended
sustenance: nourishment, means of livelihood

But Herman was *pertinacious* in his belief that he appeared more mysterious, than unpleasant.

TEND/TENS/TENT/TENU: to stretch, to thin (Latin)

tension: the act of stretching or straining
tentative: of the nature of, or done as a trial, attempt
tendentious: having a predisposition towards a point of view
distend: to expand by stretching
attenuate: to weaken or reduce in force
extenuating: making less serious by offering excuses

He grew mildly *contentious* when told he was wrong.

THEO: god (Greek)

atheist: one who does not believe in a deity or divine system
theocracy: a form of government in which a deity is recognized as the supreme ruler
theology: the study of divine things and the divine faith

Herman felt he was the *apotheosis* of a "masked man."

TRACT: to drag, to pull, to draw (Latin)

tractor: a powerful vehicle used to pull farm machinery
attract: to draw either by physical force or an appeal to emotions or senses
contract: a legally binding document
detract: to take away from, esp. a positive thing
abstract: to draw or pull away, remove
tractable: easily managed or controlled

Eventually no one argued with him because it would have become a *protracted* affair.

TRANS: across (Latin)

transaction: the act of carrying on or conduct to a conclusion or settlement
transparent: easily seen through, recognized, or detected
transition: a change from one way of being to another
transgress: to violate a law, command, or moral code
transcendent: going beyond ordinary limits
intransigent: refusing to agree or compromise

Herman's self image was unfortunately not *transitory* and so eventually there was no one left in his life with whom he could have any conversation at all.

US/UT: to use (Latin)

abuse: to use wrongly or improperly
usage: a customary way of doing something
usurp: to seize and hold
utility: the state or quality of being useful

Linda's mom took one look at the huge cork board hanging in her daughter's dorm and exclaimed, "How *utilitarian*!"

VEN/VENT: to come/to move/toward (Latin)

convene: to assemble for some public purpose
venturesome: showing a disposition to undertake risks
intervene: to come between disputing factions, mediate
contravene: to come into conflict with

She then proceeded to *circumvent* the day's visiting schedule, heading straight for the library.

VER: truth (Latin)

verdict: any judgment or decision
veracious: habitually truthful
verisimilitude: the appearance or semblance of truth
verity: the state or quality of being true

"The *verity* of the situation is that I hate guided tours," she announced.

VERS/VERT: to turn (Latin)
> *controversy:* a public dispute involving a matter of opinion
> *revert:* to return to a former habit
> *diverse:* of a different kind, form, character
> *aversion:* dislike
> *introvert:* a person concerned primarily with inner thoughts and feelings
> *inadvertent:* unintentional
> *covert:* hidden, clandestine
> *avert:* to turn away from

Linda, being an *extrovert*, happily trailed after her mother inviting other students to join them.

VI: life (Latin)
> *vivid:* strikingly bright or intense
> *vicarious:* performed, exercised, received, or suffered in place of another
> *viable:* capable of living
> *vivacity:* the quality of being lively, animated, spirited
> *joie de vivre:* joy of life (French expression)

They made a *convivial* group.

VID/VIS: to see (Latin)
> *evident:* plain or clear to the sight or understanding
> *video:* the elements of television pertaining to the transmission or reception of the image
> *adviser:* one who gives counsel to
> *survey:* to view in a general or comprehensive way
> *vista:* a view or prospect

Linda's mother considered herself a *visionary.*

VOC/VOK: to call (Latin)
> *vocabulary:* the stock of words used by or known to a particular person or group
> *advocate:* to support or urge by argument
> *equivocate:* to use ambiguous or unclear expressions
> *vocation:* a particular occupation
> *avocation:* something one does in addition to a principle occupation
> *vociferous:* crying out noisily
> *convoke:* to call together
> *invoke:* to call on a deity

This is why she made the *provocative* suggestion that they all join hands and dance in the library lobby.

VOL: to wish (Latin)

voluntary: undertaken of one's own accord or by free choice
volunteer: one who offers his or her services of his or her own accord
malevolent: characterized by or expressing bad will
benevolent: characterized by or expressing goodwill

Linda, of her own *volition*, decided it was time to say goodbye.

come to us for the best prep

about KAPLAN

EDUCATIONAL CENTERS

"How can you help me?"

From childhood to adulthood, there are points in life when you need to reach an important goal. Whether you want an academic edge, a high score on a critical test, admission to a competitive college, funding for school, or career success, Kaplan is the best source to help get you there. One of the nation's premier educational companies, Kaplan has already helped millions of students get ahead through our legendary courses and expanding catalog of products and services.

"I have to ace this test!"

The world leader in test preparation, Kaplan will help you get a higher score on standardized tests such as the SSAT and ISEE for secondary school, PSAT, SAT, and ACT for college, the LSAT, MCAT, GMAT, and GRE for graduate school, professional licensing exams for medicine, nursing, dentistry, and accounting, and specialized exams for international students and professionals.

Kaplan's courses are recognized worldwide for their high-quality instruction, state-of-the-art study tools and up-to-date, comprehensive information. Kaplan enrolls more than 150,000 students annually in its live courses at 1,200 locations worldwide.

"How can I pay my way?"

As the price of higher education continues to sky-rocket, it's vital to get your share of financial aid and figure out how you're going to pay for school. Kaplan's financial aid resources simplify the often bewildering application process and show you how you can afford to attend the college or graduate school of your choice.

KapLoan, The Kaplan Student Loan Information Program,* helps students get key information and advice about educational loans for college and graduate school. Through an affiliation with one of the nation's largest student loan providers, you can access valuable information and guidance on federally insured parent and student loans. Kaplan directs you to the financing you need to reach your educational goals.

"Can you help me find a good school?"

Through its admissions consulting program, Kaplan offers expert advice on selecting a college, graduate school, or professional school. We can also show you how to maximize your chances of acceptance at the school of your choice.

"But then I have to get a great job!"

Whether you're a student or a grad, we can help you find a job that matches your interests. Kaplan can assist you by providing helpful assessment tests, job and employment data, recruiting services, and expert advice on how to land the right job. Crimson & Brown Associates, a division of Kaplan, is the leading collegiate diversity recruiting firm helping top-tier companies attract hard-to-find candidates.

Kaplan has the tools!

For students of every age, Kaplan offers the best-written, easiest-to-use books. Our growing library of titles includes guides for academic enrichment, test preparation, school selection, admissions, financial aid, and career and life skills.

Kaplan sets the standard for educational software with award-winning, innovative products for building study skills, preparing for entrance exams, choosing and paying for a school, pursuing a career, and more.

Helpful videos demystify college admissions and the SAT by leading the viewer on entertaining and irreverent "road trips" across America. Hitch a ride with Kaplan's Secrets to College Admission and Secrets to SAT Success.

Kaplan offers a variety of services online through sites on the Internet and America Online. Students can access information on achieving academic goals; testing, admissions, and financial aid; careers; fun contests and special promotions; live events; bulletin boards; links to helpful sites; and plenty of downloadable files, games, and software. Kaplan Online is the ultimate student resource.

KAPLAN

Want more information about our services, products,
or the nearest Kaplan educational center?

HERE

Call our nationwide toll-free numbers:

1–800–KAP–TEST

(for information on our live courses, private tutoring and admissions consulting)

1–800–KAP–ITEM

(for information on our products)

1–888–KAP–LOAN*

(for information on student loans)

Connect with us in cyberspace:
On **AOL**, keyword **"Kaplan"**
On the Internet's World Wide Web, open **"http://www.kaplan.com"**
Via E-mail, **"info@kaplan.com"**

Write to:
Kaplan Educational Centers
888 Seventh Avenue
New York, NY 10106